UNDERSTIG
SOCIAL CARE

Second Edition

Neil Thompson
and Sue Thompson

RHP

Russell House Publishing

In Association With

First Edition published in 2002 by:
Russell House Publishing Ltd.

This Second Edition published in 2007 by:
Russell House Publishing Ltd.
4 St. George's House
Uplyme Road
Lyme Regis
Dorset DT7 3LS

Tel: 01297-443948
Fax: 01297-442722
e-mail: help@russellhouse.co.uk
www.russellhouse.co.uk

British Library Cataloguing-in-publication Data:

A catalogue record for this book is available from the British Library.

ISBN: 978-1-905541-09-6

Typeset by TW Typesetting, Plymouth, Devon
Printed by Biddles Ltd, King's Lynn

Russell House Publishing

Russell House Publishing aims to publish innovative and valuable materials to help managers, practitioners, trainers, educators and students.

Our full catalogue covers: social policy, working with young people, helping children and families, care of older people, social care, combating social exclusion, revitalising communities and working with offenders.

Full details can be found at www.russellhouse.co.uk and we are pleased to send out information to you by post. Our contact details are on this page.

We are always keen to receive feedback on publications and new ideas for future projects.

For Daniel and Mathew

The authors

Neil Thompson is an independent consultant and author with *Avenue Consulting Ltd* and Professor of Social Work and Well-being at Liverpool Hope University. He has numerous books and other publications to his name, including *Communication and Language* (Palgrave Macmillan, 2003), *People Problems* (Palgrave Macmillan, 2006) and *Power and Empowerment* (Russell House Publishing, 2006). He is series editor for the RHP Theory into Practice series of books. His website is at www.neilthompson.info.

Sue Thompson is a Director of *Avenue Consulting Ltd* and an independent social worker and mentor. She has qualifications in social work, nursing and practice teaching and is the author of *From Where I'm Sitting*, a training manual relating to working with older people (Russell House Publishing, 2002) and *Age Discrimination* (Russell House Publishing, 2005) and co-author (with Neil Thompson) of *Community Care* (Russell House Publishing, 2005).

Full size versions of the exercises

The exercises referred to at various points in the text are available free of charge in a format that can be used for making notes and for possible inclusion in a portfolio of evidence. To obtain a copy, visit www.learningcurvepublishing.co.uk and click on the 'Learning Resources Bank' tab on the menu.

Contents

Acknowledgements

We are indebted to Pauline Hallas and Sue Stansfield-Priestley for sharing with us their expertise in all matters relating to S/NVQ qualifications. We are grateful to the various participants on workshops we have run in recent years for their enthusiasm for learning and their commitment to high standards of social care practice.

Thanks are also due to Geoffrey Mann at the publishers for his support and comradeship and his faith in the quality of our work.

This book is dedicated to our young friends, Daniel and Mathew. We would like to thank them for the pleasure they have brought us in enriching our lives.

Introduction

This book has been written to provide a general introduction to the field of social care, presenting a clear overview of many of the key issues. As such, it will be of interest to anyone undertaking a course in social care, but is likely to be of particular interest to those undertaking a foundation degree or S/NVQ Level 4 in social care.

Of course, no single book can provide the underpinning knowledge base in its entirety. What is offered here more realistically is an introductory foundation to your studies. To facilitate further study there is a 'Guide to Further Learning' section at the end of the book. Here you will find suggestions for further reading as well as details of Internet resources you may wish to explore. In addition, as a further stepping stone to developing your knowledge and understanding of social care, the book is linked with another book, namely *People Skills* by Neil Thompson (2002a). This book can be used as a 'companion' to this book, a set book which helps to broaden out our understanding of many of the themes and issues covered here. From time to time, therefore, you will note a reference which suggests you consult a particular chapter from that book. It is not essential to follow up on these references to *People Skills*, but you will probably find it helpful if you do.

Working with people with social care needs is challenging and demanding. It is complex work that relies on an extensive knowledge base and a wide range of skills. This book will, we hope, go some significant way towards helping you develop a much firmer and much better developed grasp of that knowledge base. If you already have a lot of experience in working in social care you are likely to have developed quite an impressive knowledge base already. However, it is also likely that you will have developed your understanding gradually over time in a piecemeal way. This book should therefore help you link those elements of knowledge together into a more coherent and consistent framework of understanding – and thus make it easier for you to provide evidence of your understanding as part of your portfolio (gathering evidence of competence is discussed in Chapter 1). So, if you come across something you already know, don't switch off or skip to the next section. Instead, think about how this aspect of your knowledge base fits in with the others and how you can demonstrate to your assessor that you understand the issues in question. Remember that, to gain your award, you will not only have to understand the relevant issues, but also be able to *demonstrate* that you understand.

At various points in each chapter you will come across exercises. These are designed to help you think about the issues and work out your own views of them. We would strongly recommend that you complete these exercises, partly because they can be a useful way of both checking and deepening your understanding and partly because you may be able to use them as part of your portfolio of evidence to demonstrate your awareness and understanding of important issues. If you would find it helpful to have these exercises laid out in a workbook-style format, they can be downloaded free of charge from the authors' website at www.learningcurvepublishing.co.uk. The main aim of the book is to help those involved in social care to consolidate and extend their knowledge base and, while we have already mentioned its relevance for S/NVQ4 candidates and Foundation degree students, it may also be of interest and use to:

- assessors, mentors and managers with responsibility for supervising candidates pursuing the awards;
- candidates, assessors and mentors at S/NVQ Levels 2 and 3 (for parts of the book at least);
- students undertaking other courses of study in relation to social care and social work;
- anyone wanting to develop a fuller understanding of what is involved in the complex and fascinating world of social care.

Regardless of your purpose in using this book, we very much hope it will help you develop your understanding of social care and we wish you well with your efforts to do so.

A note on terminology

How we refer to the people we seek to help in social care is a complicated matter. There is no universally accepted term. Client, service user, resident, member, customer, consumer, recipient – these are all in use in different places and at different times. Service user is probably the most widely used term in social care these days, and so that is the one we have opted to use in this book. However, we accept that it is far from ideal and that some people object to it, especially when it is shortened to 'user' and has connotations of illegal drug use.

Chapter 1

Learning from Experience

1.1 Introduction

This chapter is designed to 'set the scene' for your learning journey. It describes the:

- six chapters that go to make up this book;
- process of evidence gathering and assessment;
- processes of learning and the obstacles to learning that we can encounter;
- various learning styles that people use;
- importance of integrating theory and practice;
- importance of reflective practice; and the
- process of action planning.

In this first chapter the emphasis is on preparation for learning. It is geared towards helping you understand what is involved in the process of learning, how it can go wrong or be blocked, and what can be done to make the most of the learning opportunities that become available through everyday practice and from your specific studies relating to the underpinning knowledge base. It will not give you 'magic answers' that make everything else you learn fall neatly into place, but it should help to give you a clearer picture of what is involved in the process of learning.

The second chapter is entitled *The Value Base of Social Care*. It is important to note that the value base is not a separate entity in its own right, but rather something that applies across the board and has a bearing on all aspects of your studies, and indeed of your practice more broadly. Values are a fundamental part of professional practice, and so it is important that we have a good grasp of how our values affect the work we do, the assumptions we make, and so on.

Chapter 3 concentrates on partnership and explores what is involved in collaborating effectively with service users, carers and colleagues. This is broken down into two parts. First, we look at how you interact with service users, how you form effective working relationships (for example, the 'engagement' referred to in S/NVQ Unit HSC41) so that you are able to make a reality of the notion of 'partnership'. Next, we look at partnership in the sense of multidisciplinary collaboration. We therefore explore the issues that arise in relation to working effectively and constructively with colleagues within your own organisation and outside it.

The fourth chapter concentrates on issues of assessment. The focus here is on what goes into gathering the necessary information to form a picture of the situation and decide what needs to be done – identifying problems to be solved or needs to be met and choosing the most appropriate steps to take. This chapter also includes a consideration of the process of risk assessment – working out what risk factors apply in a situation and what other important considerations there are so that situations involving risk can be handled to best effect. This refers not only to managing risk in terms of service user safety but also in contributing towards the development and maintenance of a healthy work environment for yourself and your colleagues.

Planning is the major theme of Chapter 5. In working with people in a health or social care setting, it is important to be able to plan ahead as far as is reasonably possible. There are, of course, dangers involved in simply stumbling from one situation to the next without having some sort of plan of action or an overview of the situation that allows us to anticipate potential problems and capitalise on positive opportunities.

The final chapter addresses issues of evaluation and development. This involves exploring what is involved in evaluating our work so that we can learn from it, and also what other avenues are available to us to enable us to continue to learn and consolidate our professional development rather than 'go stale' or 'get into a rut'. This heightened awareness can also help you to support others in their professional development and to foster a learning culture within your place of work.

It must be emphasised that it is certainly not the case that this book will provide you with all the information and knowledge you need. The knowledge base relevant to your work is far too great to be fitted into six chapters. The role of this book, then, is to act as a linking thread. It should provide you with:

- A basic introduction to the relevant subject areas;
- The opportunity to reflect on how your experience to date fits in with and reflects the knowledge base;
- Exercises to help you recognise and consolidate the knowledge base underpinning your work; and
- A set of guidelines on how to continue developing your knowledge and skills.

The chapters are designed to supplement, where possible, a programme of workshops, further reading and study, and supervised practice. These elements are all important:

- *The six chapters*: These should act as a linking thread and provide a pathway for you to follow.
- *Workshops*: These can provide invaluable opportunities for you to discuss your ideas with fellow workers, to explore issues, practise skills, review practice and develop confidence.
- *Further reading and study*: One of the important themes to be developed in this book is that of the need to become a reflective practitioner. This involves, amongst other things, keeping up to date with developments and broadening our understanding of the range of important social, psychological and other factors that have a bearing on our work.

- *Supervised practice*: Opportunities to learn from practice can be greatly enhanced by supervision, especially if you are lucky enough to have an experienced and skilled supervisor or mentor, or whoever has been designated by your programme as the one who facilitates your learning.

Of course, not everyone will have the good fortune to have all four of these elements in place at the same time, although it is likely that a good proportion should be able to achieve this balance.

Achieving any award in social care is not easy or straightforward, nor should it be if it is to be of value in helping you develop your competence, effectiveness and confidence. It involves a lot of hard work and commitment, but these should be repaid in full by the benefits to be gained from developing your knowledge and skills, thereby increasing opportunities for job satisfaction and success in achieving high standards of practice. These benefits should apply in both the short and long term, acting as a foundation for future learning and development. We therefore wish you luck in your efforts and hope that this book will play a constructive part in helping you in achieving your aim.

1.2 Planning your studies

How you plan or structure your studies will depend on what programme you are following: S/NVQ Level 4, a foundation degree in social care, or more informal learning. We shall comment briefly on each in turn.

S/NVQ Level 4

Where S/NVQ4 candidates are concerned, the candidate is expected to work through the requirements outlined in units that are divided into two categories, core and optional. The core units are compulsory and cannot be side-stepped or avoided in any way. They are deemed to be the fundamentals of good practice and are therefore essential for all staff seeking the award.

The core units are supplemented by a set of optional units from which candidates can choose the ones they wish to concentrate on. The overall award therefore involves a mixture of compulsory or core units and further optional ones. Appendix I provides a brief outline of the various units.

Foundation degrees in social care

While foundation degree curricula are likely to have certain features that are common to all, there will be some variation in terms of topics and priorities. You will need to look closely at the course handbook or equivalent information provided to registered students in order to be clear about what is expected of you. If in doubt ask one of the course staff.

Informal study

You may be reading this book out of general interest or to develop your understanding of what is involved in social care (perhaps because you are considering a career in this field). If that is the case, our advice would be that you read the whole book through to begin with and then go back and read in more depth those sections that particularly interest you and/or those sections where you feel you have most to learn.

1.3 Evidence gathering and assessment

Conventional courses in social work and social care are assessed primarily through written assignments and/or examinations as well as through the assessment of direct practice on placement. The philosophy behind S/NVQ, however, makes assessment a matter of gathering and presenting evidence of competence. In this regard, Level 4 is very similar to Levels 2 and 3, in so far as the main focus is on constructing a portfolio of evidence sufficient to convince assessors and verifiers that you have met the requirements for the award at this level. For a foundation degree you will need to check the specific assessment requirements for your programme.

In a portfolio your task is to put together a range of forms of evidence that help to demonstrate your competence for each of the relevant units and elements. This can include:

- Reports or other records of practice prepared in the normal course of your duties;
- Accounts of practice written specifically to be included in your portfolio of evidence;
- Direct observation of your practice by an assessor; and
- A 'reflective' diary in which you record important comments about what you did, why you did it, how you felt about it, what you learned from it, and so on.

If you have already been engaged in S/NVQ work at Level 2 or 3, then you will be very familiar with the type of process that is involved. For Level 4, there is much in common, but with at least one significant difference. It is reasonable to expect that a member of staff working towards the Level 4 Award should be able to demonstrate not only that he or she is competent at performing certain tasks or duties, but is also able to say why such tasks are important or necessary, how they fit into the overall process of social care, how they may have been done differently and so on. In addition, there is an expectation that he or she develops the skills to be able to promote good practice in others. Degree-level students too will need to take on board that social care has a context that goes far beyond their individual practice and the following issues will be relevant to both sets of people:

- *Professional accountability*: Taking responsibility for your actions and being able to justify what you did and why you did it. This does not mean that you are expected to 'cover your back' and be defensive, but it does mean that you have to think through very carefully the likely consequences of your actions. It also means that you should be clear about how your actions are underpinned by the legal and policy basis of your work. Seeing the wider picture and fostering this awareness in others, in order to enhance their professional development, is also part of the task at this level.

- *Reflective practice*: This refers to styles of practice that are based on integrating theory and practice, practising creatively and so on, rather than following routines or instructions.

- *Dealing with complexity*: Levels 2 and 3 are geared towards dealing with the day-to-day tasks and demands of social care, while staff at Level 4 can reasonably be expected to be involved in some of the more complex and challenging aspects of the job.

The process of gathering evidence should therefore take account of these higher level demands to make sure that there are no doubts associated with your ability to work at a level and standard consistent with an appropriate level for your particular qualification.

You should of course not be isolated in the process of putting together an appropriate portfolio of evidence. In addition to colleagues who may be going through the process at the same time as you are, you should have the input and guidance of an assessor who should be skilled and probably experienced in the tasks involved in gathering evidence. You are not alone!

1.4 Learning how to learn

Although everyone is capable of learning, some people are better equipped than others when it comes to taking advantage of the learning opportunities available. Indeed, some people are highly skilled, while others struggle to cope with the basics. But, the important point to note is that learning consists of a set of skills that can be developed over time with practice, persistence and application.

What this means, then, is that, if you are already a skilled learner, there is still potential for becoming even more skilled – and if, in the past, you have struggled with certain aspects of learning, all is not lost! You have the potential to develop your learning skills so that you can build on your learning to date. This section of Chapter 1 is designed to help participants understand the processes involved in learning, the barriers that can be encountered and the steps that can be taken to maximise your learning and skill development.

Active learning

The first point to emphasise is that learning is, or should be, an active process, if it is to be used to best effect. It is not unusual for us to learn things without even recognising that we are doing so, but where learning is active – that is, where we are making a deliberate effort to learn – the breadth and depth of learning can be much greater, and its positive steps can be much longer lived.

Active learning involves a degree of self-awareness – that is, being aware of our own ideas and values, our own approaches to situations. Without this self-awareness, we would not be able to think about other ways of tackling situations and so we would never learn. In other words, if we have little or no idea about how we operate when we are carrying out our duties, then there is little scope for us to change the way we operate – and, as we shall see, learning necessarily involves a degree of change.

Kolb's learning cycle

David Kolb is a psychologist whose ideas about adult learning have proved to be very influential. In particular, his concept of the learning cycle has been especially useful in helping us understand processes of learning. His basic argument is that people do not automatically learn from experience – we have to 'work on' or 'process' the experience. This involves four stages as follows:

1. **Concrete Experience**
   This can take a variety of forms. It can be an attempt at formal learning – a book, a lecture and so on – or more informal opportunities – conversations, day-to-day experiences, and so on.
2. **Reflective Observation**
   Concrete experience needs to be interpreted – we need to make sense of it. We need to ask the question of what the experience means to us and this question is what characterises the stage of reflective observation. In order to learn from our experiences, we first reflect on them and make sense of them.
3. **Abstract Conceptualisation**
   Reflective observation opens the door for a broader and deeper consideration from the issues arising from one's experience. The experience can be linked to other experiences, beliefs and attitudes and thus integrated into one's overall life experience. This entails considering the implications of the concrete experience and evaluating its relevance and validity. Such conceptualisation frequently entails forming a hypothesis or 'working model' of the situation.
4. **Active Experimentation**
   This is the stage at which the hypotheses formed at the previous stage are tested out in practice. The ideas arising from the progression through the three previous stages are now tried out as the learner actively experiments with what he or she has learned (from Thompson, 2006a).

The implications of Kolb's model

This perspective on the process of learning has a number of important implications, not least the following:

1. *Active learning*: As mentioned above, learning is expected to be active. It will not necessarily happen spontaneously. We do not learn directly from experience – it is what we do with that experience that enables us to draw out the learning from it.

2. *Responsibility for learning*: Although there may well be others who are supportive of us in the process of learning (tutors, trainers, assessors, mentors, line managers, colleagues), the basic responsibility lies with the individual concerned. We are the only people who can make it happen – others can help, support and encourage, but no one can *make* us learn. We have to take the initiative and follow the process through.

3. *Learning style*: One further implication of Kolb's learning cycle is that we can work out what our preferred style of learning is. Some people prefer to stick with *concrete experience* as far as possible – they prefer doing to thinking, while others feel more comfortable with *reflective observation* – musing on what has happened and trying to make sense of it. Yet others may concentrate on *abstract conceptualisation* and 'theory building'. And finally, some may particularly enjoy *active experimentation* – trying out new ideas whenever possible. According to Kolb and his associates, the way to maximise learning is to become adept and comfortable at *all four* aspects of the learning cycle and therefore avoid 'getting stuck' by either:

   - spending too much time concentrating on our preferred style and thus taking too simplistic an approach to the complex subject of how people learn; or
   - neglecting our least favourite style – thereby restricting our learning opportunities.

We should therefore work towards ensuring that we:

- take an active approach to learning;
- become proficient at all four elements of the learning cycle; and
- take responsibility for our own learning.

Obstacles to learning

It has to be recognised that there are a number of barriers to learning that can be encountered. Such obstacles can be serious problems in preventing some people from getting the most out of their learning opportunities. Our intention here, then, is to outline a number of such obstacles to enable you to be aware of them, avoid them where possible and remove them where necessary.

Anxiety

Perhaps the most common and most important obstacle to learning is anxiety. If we become too anxious, it is likely that we will be too worried to learn. We may not notice important aspects of the situation (significant patterns or other people's responses, for example) because we are concentrating on surviving the situation without experiencing any harm or embarrassment. It is ironic that anxiety about embarrassment can lead to a 'self-fulfilling prophecy'. That is, if we are worried about making a fool of ourselves, we may become so engrossed in doing so that we lose sight of what is happening around us – and therefore increase the likelihood of doing something foolish. It is very similar as far as learning is concerned – we can be so anxious about learning that we make it virtually impossible to do so. Consider the following example.

Case example
Dave was a student on placement. He was very eager to do well and to demonstrate evidence of competence in relation to his course requirements. He was also anxious about learning, very worried that he would not be able to cope with the demands of the placement. However, at one point, Dave's practice assessor had to take him on one side and ask him to 'lighten up'. She was concerned that Dave's anxiety was preoccupying him so much that he was not able to concentrate fully on the work he was doing. Ironically, it was his anxiety about learning that was actually stopping him from learning.

Complacency
At the other extreme comes complacency. This involves adopting an attitude of overconfidence, arrogantly assuming that you are so skilled and experienced that you have nothing left to learn. Of course, the problem with this point of view is that it fails to appreciate just how complex and demanding work in social care is. There is so much to learn, and the field is also changing so fast, that it is impossible for any one individual to know all that there is to know. Such an attitude is therefore dangerous, in so far as it means the person concerned has turned his or her back on learning – and is therefore becoming steadily more out of touch with developments and the realities of practice. They continue to apply old ideas to new situations and tend not to notice that they do not fit, as they are too complacent to accept that they, like everyone else, have learning needs.

Routinisation
Just as complacency can lead to opportunities for learning being missed, so too can 'routinisation'. Of course, we all rely on routines to get us through the demands of the day, but the danger comes when we rely so heavily on routines that we do not think enough about some situations which are too complex or out of the ordinary to be handled effectively by routines. 'Routinisation' is therefore something that can get in the way of learning – an obstacle to development because our tendency to react to situations in a set, standardised way means that we do not get the chance to respond differently when this is called for – and therefore do not get the chance to learn from new situations or new ways of tackling old situations.

An important skill of learning, then, is the ability to distinguish between those activities and situations that can be dealt with in a routine way and those that need to be looked at much more closely. We need to be clear about where the boundary lies between situations that are safely handled as routines and those that are not.

Exercise 1.1

How would you distinguish between a situation that is safely handled as a routine and one that needs much more careful handling? What are the key features that would differentiate one type of situation from the other?

Boredom

Although often a direct consequence of routinisation, boredom can be an obstacle to learning in its own right. It is often the stimulation arising from the situations we deal with that gives us the motivation and energy to continue with other tasks. Consequently, if we do not get enough stimulation from what we are doing, we become bored or 'understimulated', and this can make it difficult for us to remain sufficiently interested or motivated to continue.

This can also apply to learning – if we are bored with what we are doing, we are less likely to be open to new ways of thinking and therefore far less likely to learn. At times, boredom can actually be a stimulus to learning. That is, because we are bored, we may go out of our way to find new or interesting things to do, or start to look at situations in new and interesting ways. We therefore have to recognise that boredom is not in itself an obstacle to learning – rather, it is the way we respond to boredom that can be either a help or a hindrance when it comes to learning.

Paralysis by analysis

This interesting phrase refers to the tendency that some people have to analyse a situation over and over again to the point where they spend so much time and energy thinking about it that they have nothing left over to deal with it. This may be partly another example of anxiety, where the person concerned feels comfortable thinking about a situation, but is rather nervous about actually rolling their sleeves up and dealing with it.

Whatever the causes of this tendency are, it is clearly a problem when it comes to learning. This is because learning is not a passive matter of absorbing information but rather an active process that involves trying new ideas out in practice and reflecting on our experience (as noted above in relation to the Kolb learning cycle). Paralysis by analysis can therefore be a significant obstacle to learning. It is in some ways the opposite of routinisation – too much reflection and not enough action as opposed to the use of uncritical routines with not enough reflection.

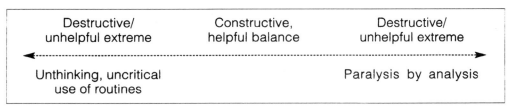

Figure 1.1 The learning balance

Lack of confidence

If we do not have faith in our ability to learn, then we are placing further obstacles in our way. Learning is something that we can all generally realise. However, if we keep saying to ourselves that we cannot learn, we just make it more difficult to do so.

A lack of confidence can also mean that we do not appreciate how much we already know or what skills we already possess. We therefore have to be very wary of adopting too negative a picture of our own abilities and potential. For many people, this lack of confidence is a legacy of their experience at school where they perhaps did not do as well as they would have liked. However, it is important to recognise that adult learning is very different from the 'fill you up with knowledge' approach that you may have experienced in school (especially if that was some time ago!), in a number of ways, including the following:

- It is geared more towards exploring ideas for yourself, rather than accepting the established wisdom. It is expected that your learning will be active.

- You are encouraged to collaborate and support each other in your learning, rather than compete with each other.

- The direction you take in your learning is largely up to you (within limits, of course).

Adult learning, then, is intended to be active, collaborative and self-directed. This means, in effect, that many people who struggled or did not achieve their potential in a school learning environment can do far better with an adult-centred approach to learning.

Sabotage

Sometimes, there are reasons why people do not want to learn. This may be for some of the reasons given here (for example, anxiety caused by feeling threatened or boredom leading to apathy). Alternatively, it may be that the person concerned is not committed to learning, and is perhaps undertaking a course of study for other reasons (to get a paper qualification, to show they are better than someone else or because they are being forced to, for example). Whatever the reason for not wanting to learn, the result is often that of 'sabotage'. That is, someone who is not committed to learning can be a 'spanner in the works' by:

- Not undertaking tasks set (for example, reading a particular text or preparing a presentation on a particular topic);

- Disrupting other people's learning (for example, by not sticking to the topic during group discussions);

- Undermining what is going on (for example, through inappropriate or excessive use of humour);

- An aggressive attitude towards others involved in the learning process.

Fortunately, such examples of sabotage are relatively rare – they are certainly not everyday occurrences. However, where they do occur, they can be very problematic indeed for all concerned.

Rejection of theory

The discussion below of integrating theory and practice shows that it is important to recognise the valuable role that theory plays in helping us understand the complex situations we encounter in social care. However, some people adopt a very negative attitude towards theoretical issues and argue that they 'prefer to stick to practice'. This tendency to reject theory is, of course, a dangerous one, as it means that we are placing barriers in the way of our own learning (much learning comes from theory and research) and we are less open to looking at situations from different perspectives (thereby running the risk of becoming dogmatic and narrow-minded). These are points to which we shall return below.

Becoming a better learner

As stated above, some people are better at learning than others. However, it can be argued that we can all become better learners – we can all develop our skills to a certain extent at least so that we can make the most of the opportunities for learning that come our way in our day-to-day lives and in our studies.

Important parts of this process of developing our learning skills are:

- having an awareness of how learning works so that we can take the necessary steps to help it happen;

- recognising the potential barriers to learning and ensuring, as far as possible, that we do not allow them to hold us back unnecessarily;

- remaining alert to the opportunities for learning that arise on a day-to-day basis (see Section 1.6 below on reflective practice).

Exercise 1.2

This exercise is an opportunity for you to think about your own learning and to identify the potential or actual obstacles you face. Which particular ones do you feel apply to you? (You may find it helpful to discuss this with a colleague or friend.) What can you do to try to make sure that these do not hold you back?

1.5 Integrating theory and practice

One of the barriers to learning identified in Section 1.4 was that of the gap between theory and practice. If people see theory and the knowledge base generally as matters unconnected with actual practice, then they are:

- Misunderstanding the relationship between theory and practice;
- Building barriers to further learning and skill development;
- Running the risk of practising *dangerously*, of doing more harm than good.

In view of this, it is important that we should explore what is involved in integrating theory and practice. The following comments are intended to provide an overview of the relationship between theory and practice.

Understanding the context

The events that take place in social care are, of course, not simply a set of coincidences or accidental occurrences; they owe a great deal to the *context* in which they occur – that is, the range of circumstances that have an influence on people's actions and attitudes. These include the following:

- *Social divisions*: Although each of us is a unique individual, we are also all parts of broader social groups or categories such as class, race/ethnicity, gender, age, disability, sexual identity and linguistic group. These social divisions play an important part in shaping our experiences and the way we are treated by other people (Thompson, 2006b). A theoretical understanding of social divisions is therefore important in order to be able to appreciate the ways in which the social context is such a significant factor in people's lives.

- *Law and policy*: Much of what happens in social care work arises from particular pieces of legislation (for example, the Children Act 1989, the NHS and Community Care Act 1990; The Disabilty Discrimination Act 1995; the Human Rights Act 1998) and the policies that have been developed in response to them. Law and policy issues are therefore important factors in shaping the way practitioners operate. All qualified staff therefore have to have at least a basic understanding of the law and policy and the principles on which they work.

- *Human development*: How we respond to people will depend to a large extent on their stage of development. For example, we would not treat a 2-year-old, a 15-year-old and a 75-year-old in exactly the same way. We would recognise that there are differences in how we would respond to them according to their age, their level of understanding, experience and so on. Understanding such matters is a matter of understanding human development and the social and psychological factors that go with it.

- *Social influences on behaviour*: In addition to the social divisions mentioned above, there are a number of other social factors that have a bearing on people's actions and interactions. These include status, social roles and expectations, family background, occupation, the media and so on.

- *Psychological influences on behaviour*: Similarly, there are a number of psychological influences that are also very significant. These include attitudes, emotions, thought processes, memory, self-esteem and so on.

And, of course, these are not entirely separate sets of issues – they interact with each other. For example, social factors can have a significant bearing on psychological factors – social rejection perhaps making a major contribution to a problem of low self-esteem.

Understanding values

Social care is not the type of occupation in which staff simply follow orders or instructions. There is an expectation that staff form professional judgements (see the discussion of assessment in Chapter 4) and develop plans of action (see Chapter 5 'Planning Responses'), rather than simply react to other people's expectations. This means that values play an essential role in guiding our actions. In deciding what to do, we will inevitably be guided by our own set of values, by what we see as important or worthwhile, what we see as right and wrong. If we are to be able to learn from our experience, we need to be aware of how values influence the choices we make and the actions we take. This is a vitally important aspect of social care, which is why Chapter 2 is devoted entirely to the subject of values in social care.

Using frameworks

Social care work is complex and demanding. It is not something that can be done effectively by following simple guidelines in a straightforward way. We have to be able to 'think on our feet' (see the discussion of 'Reflective practice' below). However, this is not to say that frameworks to guide our action are of no value at all. There are several that can be used to help us cope with the complexities of practice, as long as we use them as a basis for well-thought-out professional practice rather than as a substitute for it.

These include:

- *Systematic practice* – the three key questions that help to keep a clear focus on what is being done and why (this will be discussed in more detail in later chapters).
- *SWOT analysis* – an aid to assessment (see Chapter 4).
- *Think-Feel-Do* – a framework for understanding complex situations (see Thompson, 2002a).

It is important to emphasise that such frameworks are not intended as simple, formula solutions, but rather as examples of how theoretical knowledge and conceptual frameworks can be an important aid to practice.

Asking why

Often, in dealing with some of the more complex and intricate aspects of social care work, we need to ask 'why?' – Why is this person behaving like this? Why is this happening? Why do I feel like this? And, of course, this is where theory and the formal knowledge base come into their own, as it is generally from these sources that we derive our answers to the question: 'Why?'

It should be clear from these examples, then, that theory is important for practice. We should also note that practice is important for theory, in the sense that theory that is unconnected with the world of practice is likely to be of very limited use. Theory and practice need to 'speak to each other', rather than simply having theory informing practice as if this were a one-way street (see Thompson, 2000a, for a discussion of the relationship between theory and practice).

1.6 Developing reflective practice

'Reflective practice' is a term that has proved to be quite influential in nurse education in recent years. However, its relevance to social work and social care is now being increasingly recognised. It is therefore important to explore the notion of reflective practice in order to:

- avoid misunderstandings about its meaning and use;
- understand what is involved;
- recognise the steps to be taken to develop the skills of reflective practice.

In order to do this you should now read a section from the set book, *People Skills* (Thompson, 2002a). See Exercise 1.3 below.

Exercsie 1.3

Chapter 24 of *People Skills* explains the basics of reflective practice. You should read that chapter now and answer the following two questions:
- How does the concept of 'problem setting' apply to you in your work?
- How do you decide what the problems are that you need to give your attention to?

One of the most common misunderstandings of reflective practice is that it is simply a matter of reflecting on our actions after the event and seeing what we can learn from this – learning from our mistakes, for example. While this process clearly has some degree of value and potential benefit, it is only one small part of the overall enterprise of reflective practice.

Reflective practice involves a number of components, chiefly the following:

- *Problem setting*: Dealing with problems is not simply a matter of finding technical solutions. First of all, we need to engage in 'problem setting', getting the feel of what the problem is in all its complexity or 'messiness'.
- *Reflection-in-action*: This involves 'thinking on your feet', reflecting on what you are doing while you are doing it. This involves considerable presence of mind and the ability to concentrate hard on what you are doing without being put off in the process. This relates closely to the comments above in relation to barriers to learning, where it was argued that both an uncritical, unthinking 'robot' response and an overzealous 'paralysis by analysis' approach can hinder learning.
- *Integrating theory and practice*: As discussed earlier, there are dangers in trying to separate theory from practice. Reflective practice is premised on the notion that

theory and practice should inform each other (hence the idea of integrating theory and practice, rather than *applying* theory to practice as if it were a one-way process).

- *Reflection-on-action*: This is the type of process I referred to earlier-reflection after the event, as it were. However, it should be noted that this is not simply a mechanical process of thinking about what was done and what resulted. Rather, it is intended to be a much more active process in which you use particular techniques to analyse your practice. See the discussion below of 'Reflective techniques'.

Reflective techniques

There are a number of ways in which reflective practice can be promoted – a number of specific techniques that can be used to help develop reflective practice (for example, see Part Two of Thompson, 2006b). For present purposes, however, we shall focus on one in particular, that of the 'critical incident technique'. Based on the work of Smith and Russell (1993), this technique comprises the following steps:

1. Identify a particular incident that has occurred recently which may have produced a very strong emotional response in you or one that has made a significant impact or impression on you.
2. Consider the following three questions:
   - What happened in this incident?
   - How would you account for this?
   - What other conceptual frameworks could help us to understand this incident?
3. Use the answers to these questions as the basis of a discussion with your colleagues and/or your line manager.

This can be a very useful technique for:

- identifying the factors that subtly influence our practice;

- helping to develop our skills in analysing and understanding the complexities of practice (the 'swampy lowlands' as Schön, 1983, calls the actual demands of 'messy' practice);

- exploring the ideas and frameworks of understanding ('conceptual frameworks') that can be used to make sense of practice;

- appreciating that there is generally more than one way of understanding a situation, more than one perspective on it;

- encouraging creativity and moving away from responses based on habit.

The critical incident technique is therefore a very important example of a reflective technique, but it is, of course, not the only one – indeed, a basic principle underpinning reflective practice is the need to be creative and imaginative, rather than rely on fixed patterns. Consequently, you should try to find as many ways as possible to develop reflective practice by using your imagination and your ability to move away from simply following routines. This should not, of course, be a solitary task, but rather one that you can work together on, helping your colleagues and letting them help you so that you can benefit from each other's experience and insights. It's also so much more enjoyable to work together.

1.7 Action planning

Given that each of us is responsible for our own learning, it should pay dividends to plan ahead for that learning, to anticipate opportunities for learning and to structure our work experience in such a way that we are able to make the most of the day-to-day learning that is available to us. The chart overleaf is intended as a guide to help you become accustomed to the process of action planning for learning.

It divides learning up into four sections or elements. These are not necessarily the only four aspects of learning but they can provide a useful framework for you to take as much control over your learning through careful planning. This is not to say that you should take a rigid or mechanical approach to the process of learning, but rather that you should find it helpful to have a clear framework to help you structure your learning.

You may be able to complete the chart on your own but it will probably be easier and more successful to do it together with colleagues or with your line manager or assessor. Remember that it is not a test or a hurdle for you to jump over. It is simply intended as a useful way of planning and structuring your learning.

1.8 Conclusion

You are now coming to the end of Chapter 1. It is to be hoped that, by this stage, you are starting to form a clearer picture of what you can expect to be exploring and also what is expected of you in terms of the knowledge base that underpins social care – or at least should do if practice is to be fair and effective. This is not to say that you should have an entirely clear picture with no confusions or doubts – it will take a long time to achieve such a comprehensive understanding of what is entailed, and that is, in itself, part of the process of learning and development. You should be feeling more confident about your ability to learn.

At S/NVQ4 and degree level there will be an expectation that you take responsibility for your own learning. It should be clear by now that you cannot just sit back and wait to be given the 'answers'. What is needed is a more proactive approach in which you go out and 'make it happen'. This involves having a commitment to:

- Integrating theory and practice rather than just relying on experience, as if this somehow provides all the knowledge and awareness we need.

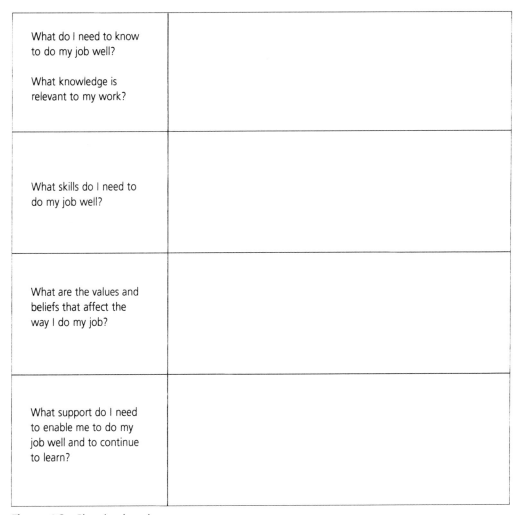

What do I need to know to do my job well? What knowledge is relevant to my work?	
What skills do I need to do my job well?	
What are the values and beliefs that affect the way I do my job?	
What support do I need to enable me to do my job well and to continue to learn?	

Figure 1.2   Planning learning

- Developing reflective practice, using reflective techniques such as the one presented in this chapter and any others that seem appropriate.

- Recognising the importance of values, and developing the sensitivity and self-awareness that are necessary to ensure that we understand how values are affecting the work we do.

Each of the chapters in the book should help to give you a clearer picture and will offer an opportunity to work on issues that you are likely to come across whichever social care course or award you are undertaking. As you continue with your studies, the picture should become less confusing as the various pieces of the jigsaw start to fit together. This is not to say that everything will be perfectly clear, with no doubts, confusions, uncertainties or gaps – that idyllic state is one that we will never reach due to the sheer complexity and constantly changing nature of social problems and social care. Part of the challenge of social care, then, is the ability to cope with uncertainty and respond positively and constructively to the changes that occur and the confusions that change can often bring about.

Chapter 2

The Value Base of Social Care

2.1 Introduction

This chapter is designed to help you think about the values that underpin the work you do in the field of social care – the principles that will guide you towards good-quality care provision. Many of the ideas will perhaps already be familiar to you, but it is to be hoped that the discussions and exercises will encourage you to think carefully about your practice and the foundations on which it is built. People come to S/NVQ and foundation degree programmes with varying levels of experience and underpinning knowledge, but there will be no one who comes with nothing left to learn. This chapter can therefore serve to reassure you about what you already know and help fill in any gaps in the knowledge required for you to be able to demonstrate that you are aware of the value base of social care and can appreciate its significance for social care practice.

It is important not to see values as something separate – an add-on to all the other areas of knowledge you need to develop – but as the *foundation* for *all* aspects of practice. The value base is an integral part of every unit in the framework and therefore an integral part of every qualification. This is because, whatever we do in social care, values play a part in shaping what we do and why we do it.

The chapter begins by looking at the definition of values before going on to explore how the following issues, chosen as representative of the value base of social care, can best be promoted:

- rights and responsibilities;
- equality and diversity; and
- confidentiality.

There will also be a section on systems and structures to show that values apply to the way teams and organisations work as well as individuals.

Within each section there will be exercises to help you integrate the general discussion into your specific work situations. These can be worked on alone or you might want to work with a colleague to share thoughts and discuss the dilemmas that arise from them.

This is followed by a brief conclusion. At the end of the book you will find a selection of suggested reading. This is designed to help you build on the necessarily limited knowledge base that this chapter is able to cover. You will no doubt be pleased to achieve your award in due course, but it is important not to think of it as the end of the learning process. Thinking in terms of continuous professional development will help to ensure that your practice continues to be grounded in up-to-date knowledge and critical reflection.

2.2 What are values?

For many people the whole concept of 'values' seems to be a very vague notion – something that is quite difficult to pin down in concrete terms. It is tempting to concentrate on more tangible things like how we behave or how we interact with one another – things we can do, observe, describe and so on – and leave thinking about values to the philosophers. However, values are such an influence on everything we do and say, how we live our lives and how we carry out our work, that we do have to engage with the subject if our practice is to have a positive impact on the lives of those for whom we provide care.

Dictionary definitions vary slightly, but essentially a value is described as something we hold dear or regard as important – in effect, something we *value*! Although we may not be consciously aware of it, we all have what is referred to as a value base. That is to say, we all live our lives in accordance with a set of principles that affect our thoughts and actions. For example, most of us respect other people's right to life and so we do not go around killing people – the sanctity of life is therefore a value which underpins most people's lives. Personal values are those which define us as an individual and influence the choices we make. As a starting point to understanding values and why they are important, try the exercise below which should help you to explore your own, personal values.

Exercise 2.1

List five views you hold dear – for example: 'Animals should have the same rights as humans'. For each one, consider how that view affects what you do or do not do in terms of: (i) what you believe; and (ii) how this affects what you do.

The concept of a value base applies not only to individuals, but also to organisations and wider communities too. For example, political parties have a value base which underpins their policies and influences their development. Some of you may be old enough to cast your minds back to the 1980s and see that Thatcherite policies on dealing with criminal behaviour were heavily influenced by a disregard for the effects of social deprivation, and relied more on an understanding of criminals as inherently 'bad' people. Policies such as 'the short, sharp shock' approach can be seen to reflect the Conservative Party's values about individual responsibility.

You might want to think about the organisation you work in. It may declare its value base very explicitly in the form of a written statement. It may just be assumed that everyone shares the same ideals, such as the right of children to grow up in secure, stimulating environments, or the right for vulnerable adults to remain in their own homes, for example. What drives your organisation? Does it make its value base explicit?

Now let us go a step further. What about whole societies? Some are premised on the superiority of men; others regard seniority rather than gender as a basis for power. Some value democracy while others accept and look to pronouncements from charismatic leaders in order to operate. Some are heavily influenced by religious values, others by more secular concerns.

We can see how values influence actions in the example of women's suffrage. At a time when women were considered to be too physically and mentally frail to engage in debates about politics and current affairs it was considered perfectly acceptable for them to be denied the right to vote in elections. Similarly, when children were considered to have no rights, it was considered acceptable for fathers and employers to mete out harsh physical punishments in the interests of supposed 'character-moulding'. What is common to both practices is the premise that men are superior to women and children. You may be able to see, then, that patriarchal (literally 'the rule of the father') values can be seen to influence how a whole society operates at a particular time.

Our own values can therefore be seen as being set in a wider context of value issues. You might have noticed that they do not always fit. For example, you may share some of the values that underpin the organisation you work for, but perhaps not all of them. Values are not necessarily static and, as organisations and individuals change, conflicting values may become apparent. You might have had experience of finding it necessary to part company with an employer or even a friend because your values were in conflict. For example, could you work for an organisation that did not value black, old, disabled or gay people?

This introductory section might not have produced a concise definition of values but should have highlighted the existence of sets of values that we all have, whether we are aware of them or not, and which influence our actions and the way we respond to people and events. Working in the care sector means that, while it is unlikely that you will share exactly the same values as someone else it is likely that you will share at least a significant number of them – for example a respect for dignity, choice and equality of opportunity. Care workers who do not care are, we hope, not the norm, and are unlikely either to apply for such work or be accepted at interview. So what are the values that act as the foundation for care work in general? Before moving on it might be useful to do Exercise 2.2, either alone or with a partner or group.

Exercise 2.2

Imagine you are the manager of a small establishment providing care for vulnerable adults or children. You are interviewing for new staff and want to ensure that your reputation as a provider of high-quality care is maintained. What values would you be looking for in the responses of the candidates? If you find this difficult, try turning it around – if you were on the receiving end of care, what values would you expect from a care worker?

There is no right answer to the exercise. That is to say, there is no absolute consensus on what constitutes the key values in care work. In any case, space does not allow for every aspect to be covered and so we have highlighted the following as being representative of high-quality social care:

- the promotion of rights and responsibilities;

- the celebration of diversity and promotion of equality; and
- the right to confidentiality.

It is to these specific values that we now turn.

2.3 Rights and responsibilities

These concepts are almost bound to feature at foundation degree level in some form and, in addition to being referred to specifically in units HSC44 and 45 of S/NVQ4, their significance is implicit throughout the whole framework of units. But what do they mean? What are rights and what do we mean by responsibilities? Why are they important and how can we promote them in our work? In order to get to grips with these questions, we need to understand that we are talking about people's rights and responsibilities as citizens of the society in which we live. Rights are about what we as citizens are entitled *to*. Responsibilities are about what is expected *of* us as citizens. Let us turn first to the concept of rights.

Rights

What are rights?
Webster's Third New International Dictionary offers the following definition: 'Something to which one has a just claim ... The power or privilege to which one is justly entitled'. Entitlement is a key issue here, in that rights are something we have a claim to as members of society – it is not a question of merit or privilege, but of fairness and equality. In the USA, citizenship rights are made explicit through legislation and, in Britain the Human Rights Act 1998 is going some way towards strengthening the status of citizenship rights. Legislation designed to challenge discrimination is also working to promote the upholding of the right of all citizens to fair treatment and equality of opportunity.

However, it is one thing being entitled to rights, it is another to be able to access those rights. In the care sector we are usually working with people in very vulnerable circumstances who may not be aware of their rights or have had them denied. If we work in a way that is insensitive to people's rights, then our practice is likely to further disempower already vulnerable people or, at the very least, miss out on the opportunity to redress the imbalance to some extent.

Before moving on to explore some specific examples, you might find Exercise 2.3 useful as a way of getting you thinking more about personal and organisational values.

Exercise 2.3

If you have been a recipient of social care services yourself, reflect on what you expected of the service. Make a list of the rights you needed to be respected. Did you feel your rights were being denied in any way? If you have no actual experience, then try to imagine the situation – put yourself in the shoes of someone for whom you are providing a service, perhaps.

Your list might have included, or will complement, the following:

Privacy
Even though we may enjoy the company of other people most of the time, there are occasions, or times of the day, when we need or want privacy. For example, we might feel unwell or upset, have bad news to deal with, secret events to plan or just want to chill out in peace! As a care worker you may be looking after people in a group setting and it is not always easy to ensure that absolute privacy is available at all times, especially if people do not have their own rooms or need constant supervision. Many cannot physically take themselves to a quiet area or communicate the wish to do so. A commitment to promoting the right to privacy and the dignity it offers should help you overcome any difficulties and heighten your sensitivity to service users' needs and wishes in this respect. In practice, there will often be a dual responsibility on your shoulders, that of respecting an individual's rights while also taking on board your responsibilities in terms of health and safety issues – you may have to find an acceptable compromise between the two.

Care work can often involve assisting with intimate aspects of personal care, such as toileting and bathing and in such situations it is not always possible to have absolute privacy. For example, a risk assessment might have highlighted the need for someone to assist a person on and off a toilet and supervise the procedure in case of falls. That should not necessarily mean, though, that the toilet door has to be left open to the view of others passing by, or that the carer remains inside the toilet area chatting about all and sundry! A simple call system or the vigilance of a care worker who stays within earshot until called to assist, could be seen to be promoting the right to privacy in a way which does not contravene the right to protection from harm.

Honesty and openness
These are rights that are closely linked with respect, and we cannot be said to be working in a respectful way if there is a lack of honesty or an underlying current of mistrust. Without an atmosphere based on openness and honesty the trust necessary for a successful working relationship between carer and service user is unlikely to flourish, which would be to the detriment of both parties. Vulnerable people often have no other option but to place their trust in the integrity of care providers and they have the right for this trust to be honoured. This can be achieved by working in partnership with service users, involving them in joint planning and keeping them informed of outcomes. This is an empowering approach which is explored in more detail in Chapter 3. It can be tempting to withhold information that could upset a service user or to delay delivering bad news, but such concern is often misguided and can lead to service users feeling betrayed and disempowered.

Case example
Ayesha is a 24-year-old woman who has mild learning difficulties and is a wheelchair user. She has lived with four other disabled people in a small group home since it became impossible, eight years ago, for her to remain living with her parents.

Although she would have preferred to stay at home, she has built up a good relationship with the other residents, who have come to rely on each other for the companionship and abilities each can offer the others. One day, without prior discussion or her opinion being sought, she is informed by her key worker that she has been allocated a highly sought-after single person apartment in another part of the city, purpose built to accommodate her wheelchair, and designed to allow her to live an independent lifestyle.

How do you think Ayesha might have felt on hearing this news? Can you identify the key worker's attitude towards disabled people from his or her actions? Would you have done things differently?

A relationship of mutual respect does not happen overnight, and is especially difficult to achieve when a service user has placed his or her trust in someone in the past and has had that trust betrayed. Working in partnership with someone – that is to say, planning and implementing goals that have been agreed on by both parties – provides a sound basis for building mutual respect based on openness and transparency, with no hidden agenda (see Chapter 3). If the ground rules about openness and honesty are set out in a spirit of partnership, then it is much more likely that those ground rules will form the foundation of a lasting and trusting relationship. You will see the term 'effective' being used quite a lot where processes are described or discussed, for example in terms of relationship building. Wherever people are involved so too is communication and this needs to be effective also if values such as respect and choice are not to be overridden by other concerns. Given the centrality of communication in social care work, we would urge you to read Chapters 10, 11 and 12 in *People Skills* (2002). Also, Neil Thompson's book, *Communication and Language* (2003a) provides a more in-depth discussion.

A voice, or representation

What do we do when we are dissatisfied with a product or service? We may not always complain or ask for some recompense, but we have a right to do so, if we choose to take it up. In this way we are able to contribute towards maintaining the standards we expect from those products or services. Users of care services also have this right but there may be instances where it may be difficult for them to make their voice heard, perhaps because of communication barriers, or lack of awareness and confidence. In such circumstances this right can be facilitated by an advocate.

It is unsettling to think that someone might complain about the service you provide, and many workers view complaints procedures in a very negative light. However, having a procedure in place to process and respond to complaints is important in a number of respects:

- It empowers vulnerable people by giving them the opportunity to have their perspective listened to by those with the power to make changes.
- It can serve to highlight areas of poor practice as issues to be discussed and reformed if necessary.

- It can act as a forum for fostering a *shared* approach to problem solving, where service users and service providers work together to produce policies.

- It can allow for good practice, as well as poor practice, to be highlighted and applauded.

Some organisations make it clear that they respect people's opinions by giving written guidance in the form of leaflets telling new service users how to complain or comment on issues of concern. Check whether this is the practice where you work and ensure that you know where to find them, or know how to set such a procedure in motion. If there is no procedure, find out how your organisation gets feedback from service users. What about those people who have communication difficulties? If you think that any individuals or groups are being disadvantaged in this respect then perhaps you could raise your concerns with your line manager or place it on the agenda for a team meeting.

Thinking a little about the above questions will have alerted you to the crucial role you can play in maintaining good standards of practice by promoting the right of service users to comment on practice as it appears from their perspective.

Respect and dignity

Human dignity is about the right to be valued as an individual with one's unique identity, and about not being demeaned or belittled, whatever anyone else feels about your beliefs or personality. You cannot expect to like or even agree with everyone with whom you come into contact but you could well be required to work with people whose beliefs differ from your own, or of whom you disapprove. It is therefore important that social care workers are *non-judgmental* – that is, that we treat everyone with dignity, not just those we like or approve of.

Unless the right to dignity becomes an integral part of your value base, it is easy to fall into the trap of 'depersonalising' service users – that is to say, treating people not as individuals but as part of a wider group, such as 'the elderly' , 'the disabled' or 'kids'. If most of the people with whom you work have, for example, mobility and memory problems, it is easy to forget that not *all* people have mobility and memory problems and that even those who do are all individuals with personalities, life experiences, problems, talents, relationships, memories, hopes and fears that are unique to them alone. If you work with young offenders who have similar histories and backgrounds, for example, you might overlook those aspects of personality and experience that makes each young person different.

Identity is closely linked to self-esteem in that identity refers to who we are – how we see ourselves and self-esteem is how we value ourselves. If we have a positive image of ourselves as individuals worthy of respect, then our self-esteem will be high, which will then feed into motivation. If our self-image is one of worthlessness, then our self-esteem will be low, and our confidence in our abilities will suffer accordingly. As a social care worker you are well placed to have a positive effect on promoting self-worth and encouraging people to see themselves as valued members of society, worthy of dignity and respect.

Protection from harm or abuse

Abuse can take many forms, but by its very definition it is something that is to be avoided. It has the potential to occur within relationships where the perpetrator holds an unequal balance of power – that is to say, when one party is more vulnerable than the other. Consider how often children, people with learning difficulties and frail older people feature in case histories of abuse, for example. Workers in the field of social care are nearly always dealing with vulnerable people, and so it is vital to ensure that we do not misuse the power we hold ourselves, albeit unwittingly, and that we are able to recognise and report abuse if we see it happening elsewhere.

The right to protection from abuse refers not just to physical harm but to other forms of abuse of power, including emotional, financial and sexual abuse. These aspects of abuse are often more difficult to detect than physical abuse but are no less devastating in their effects. For those who experience abuse, disclosing it can be difficult, or impossible, for a number of reasons. For example he or she could be:

- unable to speak or communicate in any form;
- afraid of reprisals; or
- ashamed of what has happened.

For these reasons, it is important for those working on a regular basis with vulnerable people to be vigilant to changes in mood or behaviour as well as to the more obvious signs of physical abuse. In order to protect people from abuse, there is a need to:

- accept that abuse occurs and can take many forms;
- report any concerns we have to more senior members of staff at the earliest opportunity;
- make ourselves aware of policy statements and guidelines issued by our employing organisations and ensure that we follow them in cases of suspected abuse.

Dealing with actual or potential abuse can be very difficult and demanding, and so it is important that we do not make it any harder by losing sight of the importance of values in undertaking such work.

Freedom of choice

Within certain limits prescribed by the law, the right to choose is one we exercise every day. For example, we choose what, or even whether, to eat, what to wear and how to plan our days. Being able to choose between options is part of what defines our identity as individuals and gives us a sense of being in control of our lives. But do we extend the right to choose to those people dependent on us for help and are they real choices? For example you might give someone the right to choose, but offer him or her a very limited range of options to choose from, or not provide the means for making that choice. A range of options and the opportunity to choose for oneself are both important issues here if the right to freedom of choice is not to be a tokenistic gesture, but one which recognises that those dependent on us are, like ourselves, citizens with citizenship rights.

We have referred earlier to conflicts of rights. A particularly thorny issue to consider here is that of the right of individuals to take risks, something we will explore further in Chapter 4. As far as working with adults is concerned, in most cases, you can only advise in this respect and although you have a duty to try to dissuade people from taking risks that could have harmful consequences (as in the discussion above about protection from abuse), you cannot deny them that choice, or take responsibility for their actions if harm ensues. However, there are circumstances where you *do* need to assume responsibility, and may need to look to the guidance of senior staff, such as when the person choosing to take risks is:

- a child who is judged unable to make an informed judgement about the risk, and therefore the right to choose is overruled by the right to be protected from harm.
- indulging in self-harming behaviour which implicates others and puts them at risk of harm also.
- has impaired judgement because of a mental disorder or severe learning disability.

This is a fairly long list of rights that are very relevant to social care, but even this is not a comprehensive list, or indeed anywhere near comprehensive. It should none the less be sufficient to clarify how complex values and rights are and just how relevant they are to social care practice.

Responsibilities

In addition to rights, we have to recognise the importance of responsibilities. Indeed, the two generally go together in so far as one person's right is another person's responsibility. For example, a service user's right to respect and dignity places a responsibility on other people to treat him or her with respect and dignity.

However, responsibilities do not just lie with staff. All citizens have responsibilities, and so we need to recognise not only the rights but also the responsibilities that service users have. Indeed, to ignore such responsibilities can be quite problematic. For example, in working with children and young people, not helping them to handle responsibility can be seen as doing them more of a disservice than a service. Similarly, in working with adults, to act as though they have no responsibilities may actually be quite oppressive – in effect treating them as less than fully human or as second-class citizens.

It is therefore important to consider what responsibilities the people we work with have and how we can help them exercise those responsibilities. Indeed, we could see this as an important part of empowerment – helping people gain greater control over their lives.

2.4 Equality and diversity

Introduction

As good practice is about 'starting from where the person is at', there is a need to promote equality of opportunity and the valuing of diversity if we are to play a part in challenging the adversity most service users face. Once again, let us begin this section by defining the terms.

Equality is not easy to define, as it can have several meanings. In this context it refers to people having equal rights, as citizens, to a fair share of resources and opportunities and to a social system that does not marginalise certain groups of people by pushing them to the edge of mainstream society. It can therefore be understood as meaning equal fairness. It does not mean that everyone should be the same or that resources should be shared equally, but rather that powerful groups should not be able to deny opportunity and status to those with little or no voice.

Diversity refers to difference and variety. Difference can be interpreted in a negative sense, as a problem to be addressed (somebody who is different may be seen as 'abnormal'), or in a positive way, as something to be valued (difference and variety as a source of enrichment). In this context difference is viewed as an asset, and diversity celebrated as something that adds an extra positive dimension to society rather than divides it. Thompson (2003b) refers to the management of diversity as:

> . . . *a relatively new approach and can be seen, in some ways at least, as a response to feelings of dissatisfaction with conventional equal opportunities strategies. This new emphasis, then, is on building positives, rather than seeking simply to eradicate or reduce negatives.*
>
> (p. 195)

We shall return to this important topic of diversity below.

In seeking to affirm diversity and promote equality, we need to recognise that we live in a society that is characterised by inequality and oppression, where some groups of people are disadvantaged in relation to others in such aspects as wealth and life opportunities. In the field of social care we are often working with people who have been oppressed or pushed to the margins of society, discriminated against because of their age, gender, class, ethnic group, physical or intellectual ability, religion or sexual orientation or a combination of these.

Because of this, we are in a prime position to be able to recognise and, perhaps more importantly, to challenge discrimination and oppression – that is, to practise in *anti-discriminatory* ways. Before moving on to look at how discrimination operates in its many different forms and at pointers for good practice, we must be sure we understand why it is so important that we take anti-discrimination seriously and make it a part of our value base.

Why is anti-discriminatory practice important?

There are several reasons why we need to incorporate anti-discrimination measures into the value base of social care:

- We are required to do so by law. Discrimination is illegal – see the section on suggested reading for guidance on relevant materials that explain our legal obligations.

- We cannot claim to be a caring profession that believes in social justice if we condone oppression and discrimination in any form.
- We are well placed to take up opportunities to influence opinion and challenge the negative stereotypes that have built up about particular groups of people.
- We are unlikely to be able to work effectively with people if we are condoning or reinforcing discrimination and oppression. This is no basis on which to build trust and positive working relationships.

How does discrimination operate?

Generally people tend to see discrimination as a form of prejudice or bigotry. However, we have to be careful not to oversimplify matters here. While personal prejudice is very important as a factor in causing discrimination, it is certainly not the only one. Discrimination can also be seen to operate at two other levels: cultural and structural (see Thompson, 2006b, for a fuller discussion of these issues).

The cultural level refers to what can be described as 'shared meanings' – the things we take for granted, the unwritten rules and assumptions, common images and stereotypes, and so on. Being part of a group means that we have certain ideas, beliefs and values in common, and this is what is meant by the cultural level. Discrimination operates at this level in a number of ways:

- *Language*: The language we use is often implicitly discriminatory, even if we do not intend it to be. It can:
  - ○ exclude certain groups – using terms like 'chair*man*' which promote the message that positions of power belong to men;
  - ○ demean certain people – referring to older people as 'old dears';
  - ○ 'depersonalise' people – lumping people together in one category instead of recognising them as a diverse group of individuals: 'the elderly';
  - ○ stigmatise individuals or groups – using 'black' to mean 'bad': a black day, a black mark and so on
- *Humour*: Some forms of humour are profoundly discriminatory, as they often rely on presenting one or more groups of people in an unduly negative light. This reinforces the negative views and is therefore a powerful force in maintaining discrimination in society.
- *Stereotypes*: We often make generalisations about people and things – indeed we generally have to do so a lot of the time to make sense of the complex world we live in. However, such generalisations become very problematic when we stick by them even when we have evidence to the contrary. We therefore have to be very wary of the power of stereotypes to distort reality.

The significance of the cultural level of discrimination is that it operates very subtly – we are so used to the 'shared meanings' on which it is based that we generally do not notice that it is affecting us, our actions, attitudes and decisions.

The structural level refers to the structure of society and the power relations on which it is built. That is, society is divided up in such a way that certain groups in society have more power than others. Less powerful groups are therefore more prone to being discriminated against by virtue of their relative lack of power – members of ethnic minorities, for example. In this respect, inequality is 'sewn in' to the fabric of society.

Clearly, then, discrimination is much more than just personal prejudice – it is a complex set of issues that operate at personal, cultural and structural levels. One of the implications of this is that outcomes are more important than intentions. That is, while we may not intend to discriminate, if a particular individual or group is discriminated against, then the outcome is one that we should seek to avoid. Saying that we did not intend for somebody to be disadvantaged unfairly does not alter the fact that they have been discriminated against. We therefore have to be very careful to ensure that the outcomes of our actions are fair and non-discriminatory. Good intentions are not enough.

This does not mean that we should feel guilty about discrimination, as feelings of guilt and blame can easily emotionally paralyse people to such an extent that they are not thinking clearly or acting rationally – and that in turn can lead to more discrimination. So, it is not a matter of owning up to being discriminatory, but rather of being open and flexible enough to take responsibility for learning about discrimination, how to avoid it and how to tackle it – a case of *taking ownership* rather than *owning up*.

Forms of discrimination

Anyone can experience oppression, or be discriminated against at some point in their lives, but for some social groups – for example black, disabled, or older people – it is something that is much more likely to be experienced and at a level that is deep rooted and pervasive. That is to say, it is often experienced in the form of lower standards of health care, educational facilities and so on, as well as at the level of personal insult and assumptions of inferiority.

Space does not allow us to look at every oppressed group or in any great detail in the discrimination that occurs, and so we have chosen to concentrate on the more well-established examples. You may then be able to apply the themes and principles that emerge to an understanding of other areas of discrimination you might encounter.

Racism
Racism is about categorising people into assumed biological groups, based on skin colour and other physical characteristics, and then going on to assume that certain of these groups are inferior to others on the basis of those biological characteristics. Pilkington (2003) defines racism as:

> . . . a discourse which involves four features: identifying groups, which reproduce themselves over time, on the basis of physical markers; seeing essential differences between them; associating others with negative characteristics; and visualising the dissolution of boundaries as undesirable.

> (p. 189)

So, for example, it allows for negative stereotypes such as 'Irish people are stupid' and 'black people are lazy' to flourish. In this way it works to hide the rich diversity of experience, personality and individuality within different groups, rather than to celebrate or affirm it.

As we discussed earlier, discrimination can take different forms, ranging from insults at a personal level to, for example, disproportionately harsh treatment in the penal system at the structural level. It is not enough to say 'I don't behave in a racist way and therefore absolve myself of all responsibility'. If we do not take up the opportunities offered to us to challenge discriminatory behaviour by other individuals or organisations, we are doing those for whom we provide care a disservice by condoning systems that perpetuate racist attitudes and practices. The exercise below should help you think about racism and what you can do to counter its effects.

Exercise 2.4

1. How would you describe your own racial or ethnic background? Can you identify ways in which this is significant (for example, in terms of how individuals, groups or organisations treat you or expect you to behave)?
2. Imagine you were a member of a different ethnic or racial group. What differences to your life would it make? Would people treat you any differently?
3. As an individual working in a social care context, what can you do to make sure that ethnic differences are seen in a positive light rather than a source of discrimination and disadvantage? Take some time to discuss this with your colleagues – it is not an easy question to answer.

Disablism

Disablism refers to the ways in which people with physical or intellectual impairments are seen in terms only of what they cannot do and are treated in an inferior way because of this negative stereotyping. Wheelchair access to public transport and buildings has long been given scant attention and few buildings incorporate the technology available to allow deaf people to participate in public meetings. Oliver (1996) comments that:

> *It is true that disabled people have been systematically excluded from British society; they have been denied inclusion into their society because of the existence of disabling barriers.*

(p. 158)

This approach can be described as a *social* model of disability. That is to say, it is one which highlights that it is the way in which society is geared towards the needs of 'able-bodied' people that leads to the disadvantages experienced by disabled people, rather than the physical impairment itself being the main problem. Despite some progress since his earlier comment, Oliver still felt the need to comment eight years on:

I have argued that the social model of disability is a practical tool, not a theory, an idea or a concept. Further, I have suggested that we have spent too much time discussing it rather than attempting to use it to produce social and political change.

(2004, p. 11)

In a similar vein, in the same publication, Sapey comments on how the unequal power relations between disabled and non-disabled people does not seem to have been challenged significantly, despite hopes that the post-industrial 'information society' might make it easer for disabled people to compete in the modern economy.

Working with disabled people incorporates managing varying degrees of dependency. Part of your job is to provide 'care'. But if you are not to fall into the trap of perpetuating the oppression of disabled people it is important to recognise the right that disabled people have to be treated as citizens with equal rights rather than as 'pathetic' victims of circumstance or as objects of charity. A social care approach that looks at how people with disabilities can be assisted to take as much control over their lives as possible is one that will be effective in challenging discrimination, whereas one that provides care in a very paternalistic way will only serve to perpetuate it.

Exercise 2.5

If you work with disabled people, how do you ensure that as much control as possible is exercised by the service user? Do you encounter problems in this respect when outside of the immediate work environment? If you do, how might these problems be overcome?

Sexism

Gender inequality is so deeply ingrained in our society that we often fail to notice it – we have become so accustomed to it. One of the main ways in which it works is for certain roles (at home or in the workplace) to be automatically associated with a particular gender. For example, caring roles are strongly associated with women. This can mean that women feel under a great deal of social pressure to undertake caring duties, while men may feel under pressure not to (because caring is not seen as 'masculine'). It is therefore important to ensure that people do not lose out on opportunities based on assumptions about gender. Rigid gender roles can be quite a straightjacket for all concerned.

Ageism

As with disabled people, older people are often portrayed as 'unfortunates', in need of care and charitable concern, rather than as individual people with the same range of life experience, interests, abilities and problems as any other group of people. Although advancing age is associated with a higher incidence of disability and illness (Sue Thompson, 2005) to assume that *all* older people are frail and dependent is to accept the prevalent negative stereotype perpetuated by, for example, advertising images and portrayals of older people in television programmes. Hughes (1995) describes ageism as:

> ... a matrix of beliefs and attitudes which legitimates the use of age as a means of identifying a particular social group, which portrays the members of that group in negative, stereotypical terms and which consequently generates and reinforces a fear of the ageing process and a denigration of older people.
>
> (p. 43)

Ageism is most often used to refer to discrimination on the grounds of old age, but can also be seen to apply to the stereotyping of young people, for example in the tendency to describe all teenagers as rebellious. Basing your attitudes and actions on assumptions fuelled by stereotypes is something you should avoid if you are serious about promoting equality. You can contribute to the denigration referred to above or play a part in challenging it. Recognising ageist assumptions in your own practice and that of others is a step towards ensuring your practice is one that incorporates the promotion of equality as a valid and important concept.

As mentioned earlier, one way in which ageism manifests itself is in the use, and toleration of, demeaning language. Although probably not intended as such, use of terminology such as 'dear' or 'pet', or the practice of addressing older people by their first names without checking whether that is their preferred title, or children and young people by nicknames, can serve to make them feel patronised and undeserving of respect – the message being that they are 'less than' adults who are not at either extreme of the age spectrum and would expect this respect as a matter of course. So too can making decisions on behalf of people on the assumption that they do not have the capacity to participate, that assumption being made purely on the basis of their age rather than on their competence. If you care for people in a group context think a little about how decisions that affect everyone are made. Who decides on the daily menus, for example? What about decor and outings? Who decides whether the television or radio is on in communal areas?

Clearly, then, there are various forms of discrimination that can apply in a social care context, plus many more that we do not have the space to discuss here. The key point to recognise, in our view, is that any unfair discrimination – on whatever grounds it operates – needs to be tackled. At the very least we should not condone or reinforce existing discrimination through our own actions and attitudes, but we should also consider what steps we can reasonably take to counter and undermine such discrimination and the oppression it brings about.

Diversity

The term 'diversity' is one which has become more and more established in recent years. At its simplest level, it refers to the fact that we live in a 'diverse' society – that is, one that is characterised by various differences (different cultures, different gender perspectives, different groups of people with different needs and values and so on). As noted above, it is seen as a positive term – that is, diversity is something we should be grateful for. We should appreciate the enrichment it brings and not see differences as problems to be solved, but rather as strengths to be built upon. However, we have to recognise that there are barriers to seeing diversity in this light, obstacles to affirming diversity. These include the following:

- *Assumption of homogeneity*: This refers to the tendency to assume that people are more or less the same, that any differences are of minor significance. It is a tendency to play down differences between individuals and between groups of people. For example, a residential home catering primarily for white people may not take account of the fact that black residents may have different needs, customs or interests.

- *Equating difference with inferiority*: This involves making the false assumption that anyone or anything that is different from the mainstream is inferior or even a problem of some kind. For example, someone whose tastes are considered unusual may be thought of as 'odd' and therefore excluded in some ways.

- *Ethnocentricity*: The term 'ethnocentricity' refers to the tendency to see situations from the perspective of one's own culture or background and fail to take account of the fact that we live in a multicultural society. 'Our' way of seeing the world or of conducting ourselves within it is not the only one, and we should not be intolerant of different views, perspectives or sets of beliefs. To think or act in an ethnocentric way is to rely on the view that our own way of seeing the world is the 'correct' one, and therefore that other views are necessarily wrong.

- *Fear of the unknown*: Often people can feel irrationally threatened by difference – seeing someone with a different background as a threat. We have to be careful to ensure that feelings are not allowed to lead to discrimination.

- *Marginality of social problems*: A failure to appreciate the diversity of modern society is also a failure to recognise how significant social problems are, and how problems such as poverty and abuse are generally far more widespread than people realise.

The notion of 'promoting' or affirming diversity is therefore one that has much in common with the promotion of equality and the development of anti-discriminatory practice. The two approaches are very much geared towards the same aims. There are, however, some differences:

- Less reliance on a legalistic approach – affirming diversity involves much more than implementing equal opportunities laws.

- All staff in an organisation are encouraged and supported in maximising their potential – diversity is seen as an asset.

- Organisational culture is seen as an important factor – the way organisations work will either support or inhibit the affirmation of diversity.

- Differences are seen as positive, rather than something to be tolerated or simply accepted.

The basic idea is that, as social care workers, we should acknowledge that we live in a diverse society and should aim to affirm or even celebrate the fact that there are so many differences between people, rather than try to iron out such differences by encouraging uniformity or too narrow a view.

2.5 Confidentiality

Why is it important?

Respect for confidentiality is one of the fundamental values of social care and applies to every aspect of the work we do. It links closely to other important values, such as the right to dignity and respect. As a social care worker you will be party to personal and often highly sensitive information and owe service users a duty to deal with that information appropriately. The consequences of not doing so can be devastating in terms of the effect it can have on relationships built on trust and mutual respect. The damage can extend further than the immediate relationship between the member of staff and service user concerned. Feelings of betrayal, humiliation and powerlessness can run very deep and can lead to a mistrust of *all* staff, especially if they are experienced within a context of already feeling undervalued or vulnerable for a variety of other reasons. For these reasons, confidentiality is something that is likely to feature on most social care courses in some form. For example, S/NVQ4 candidates will be able to see that, while the wording of unit HSC41, which deals with communication, and HSC44 and HSC45, which discuss choice, protection and well-being, do not include the word 'confidentiality' specifically, they do make reference to *effective* communication and engagement, and to respect and protection. We would suggest that the importance of maintaining confidentiality is implicit in such instances, and needs to be respected if people receiving care and support are not to be disadvantaged.

Maintaining confidentiality is not always as easy or as clear cut as it sounds. For example, there are instances when maintaining confidentiality conflicts with other aspects of our value base, such as the right to protection from harm (to which we will return later). You may well be working in a multidisciplinary setting or deal with a variety of other professionals who hold information about service users, or seek it from you. When asked to share information, you can be placed in the situation of having to consider both service users' best interests and their rights. But, despite the difficulties, you can still strive to maintain confidentiality as far as possible. Respect for privacy and dignity should lead to a commitment to maintaining confidentiality as a general principle, thereby contributing to the provision of high-quality care built on a foundation of respect. We will look later on at policies and strategies that will help to build on that commitment and guide us through dilemmas that can occur during the course of our day to day work.

Whilst the need to ensure that our work is underpinned by a sound value base is incentive enough to respect confidentiality, we must remember that we are also governed by legislation. For example, storage of information is something most of us are involved in, making us subject to the Data Protection Act 1998, particularly if the information is held on computerised databases, or is collected with that intention in mind. As we can see, not taking confidentiality seriously can have legal as well as moral consequences and is therefore another reason why it is an important issue.

What do we mean by confidentiality?

We have already identified that confidentiality is a complex issue. Biestek talked about confidentiality when writing in 1961 and, while you may not be a caseworker yourself, many of the issues he discussed continue to be relevant and to provoke debate in social care practice in general. He refers to confidentiality as:

> . . . the preservation of secret information concerning the client which is disclosed in the professional relationship. [It] is based upon a basic right of the client . . . an ethical obligation of the caseworker . . . Moreover, the client's secret is often shared with other professional persons . . .

(p. 121)

However, if we start to unpack the definition a little we can reveal some of the complexities in what seems to be a fairly straightforward definition.

Let us consider 'secrecy', for example. A secret is something that you do not want to share or have shared further. But, having a secret disclosed to you can often pose a dilemma if it is something you know the discloser does not want you to pass on, but is also something which you feel *should* be passed on in the interests of preventing negative consequences. Deciding on who should be party to 'secret' information can be a difficult process, but you should be guided by an understanding that secrecy is not an absolute concept – there are instances when it can be overruled by other considerations. Banks (2005), in highlighting the dilemma inherent in having a duty to maintain confidentiality but also to protect service users, reminds us that along with duty comes accountability.

A policy of honesty with service users about our own obligations in terms of a duty to care and protect, as well as a duty to maintain confidentiality, should help prevent misunderstandings about intentions. For this reason it is important to refrain from making promises about keeping secrets, which we may then have to break in certain circumstances.

Biestek refers to confidentiality as a *basic right*. We have discussed rights earlier, and confidentiality ranks highly in the list of rights we would wish to promote. As we have seen, it does not always fit neatly with other rights we would wish to uphold. However, if we have managed to build up a relationship built on trust and a respect for dignity, by being open and honest about the boundaries of what we are allowed to keep secret, then that relationship will more easily bear the breaking of a confidence if it should become necessary.

When information is disclosed, we are often working at an individual level, but, in terms of confidentiality, we need to remember that the information is confidential to the agency who employs you, rather than to you as an individual. You will know that co-workers also have access to information you hold, but this can cause problems if service users are not also aware of this. *Sharing of information* therefore has to be incorporated into a working definition of confidentiality, but poses questions about how widely the information needs to be shared and for what purpose.

As we can see, defining confidentiality is not as easy as it sounds. The further we delve into the definition, the more complex it seems to be, and the more dilemmas it throws up. In such circumstances, agency policies can provide us with a guiding hand. Work through the exercise below to ensure that you are aware of your responsibilities in terms of confidentiality procedures.

Exercise 2.6

- As a newly appointed worker, was the issue of confidentiality discussed with you?
- Does your employer have a written policy on confidentiality? Does the policy make it clear what your responsibilities are?
- If there are no written guidelines, are you clear about the circumstances in which you are allowed to divulge information and to whom? For example, are you clear about who has access to written records?

Respecting confidentiality is a vital part of good practice, but can sometimes get overlooked in situations of panic or when things get really hectic. For this reason it is important to work hard at ensuring that a respect for the right to confidentiality underpins your practice. If you do not have the answers to the questions in Exercise 2.6, then ask a senior colleague or line manager to discuss confidentiality with you. If you have respect for service users as equal citizens then it cannot be just an optional extra.

When is it appropriate to override confidentiality?

This is a difficult question to answer. Values issues very rarely have a definitive answer because of the dilemmas inherent in them. It is perhaps useful to think in terms of guiding principles. The right to confidentiality is such an important one, for reasons which we have already discussed, that it should be observed unless, in doing so, the safety of the individual concerned (or others) is compromised. The following case study highlights such a dilemma. You might find it useful to make a few notes about how you might feel and act in such a situation.

Practice example

Paul, aged 13, has been living in a small group home, supervised by Mel and her staff of support workers. Since moving there after a history of aggressive behaviour towards staff and other residents, he has settled well and has begun to confide in Emma about his feelings and the difficulty he has in managing them. He is embarrassed about sharing his feelings but appears to trust Emma to keep the discussions confidential and, since he has been able to share how upset and lonely he gets at times, his behaviour and mood have improved considerably. On one occasion Paul discloses to Emma that he hates his father because of the emotional bullying he had experienced prior to coming into care. He tells Emma that he has received a letter from his younger brother, who has confided in Paul that their father is physically abusing both him and their mother. Paul's brother has asked him not to disclose this to anyone else. Emma does not want to destroy the relationship of trust that she has built up with Paul over a long period, but feels that the information about the father's behaviour should be shared. She decides to discuss her dilemma with her line manager the next day. That evening Paul absconds, after leaving a note to say that he had 'family business to sort out'.

Disclosure of suicide plans also poses a dilemma for workers who are told this in confidence. It is one of those situations when the right to protection is more important than the right to confidentiality. This has been recognised formally in terms of actual or supposed harm to children, in the form of child protection procedures, which impose *obligations* on us to override confidentiality. It is to be hoped that similar procedures will eventually be in place to offer protection to other groups of people who are vulnerable to abuse, such as older people and those with severe learning difficulties. It is therefore important that you keep up to date with any obligations that new policies place on you in this respect. If you find yourself in a dilemma, do not carry the burden on your own. Even if you do have written guidelines or procedures to refer to, breaking a confidence can still be a difficult thing to do, even if you know you have to. Choosing the wrong option can have serious consequences, for both service users and workers, so discuss matters with your line manager whenever you are unsure.

Figure 2.1 should help to clarify at least some aspects of the situation.

Keeping records

Record keeping is vitally important in social care. It allows knowledge about service users to be accessible to co-workers and managers, thereby facilitating continuity of care. It also ensures accountability and makes it possible for evaluation of standards to take place. But the act of recording necessarily poses problems in terms of confidentiality. Consider the following:

Which aspects of a service user's background and experience should be recorded? The short answer to this is: only what is relevant. As Neil Thompson (2002a) puts it, focus on the minimum necessary, not the maximum available. Some organisations will have designed forms to make the gathering of information more relevant and focused, but try not to be led into seeing recording information as a purely bureaucratic procedure. A useful approach is to consider *why* a specific piece of information or history is being recorded. If no purpose can be identified then you need to ask yourself whether it needs to be documented at all. Sharing this process with service users can help them to understand the rationale behind the gathering and storage of information – who will have access to it, what use will be made of it and so on. Making the process transparent to the service user will help to promote the atmosphere of trust to which we have already referred.

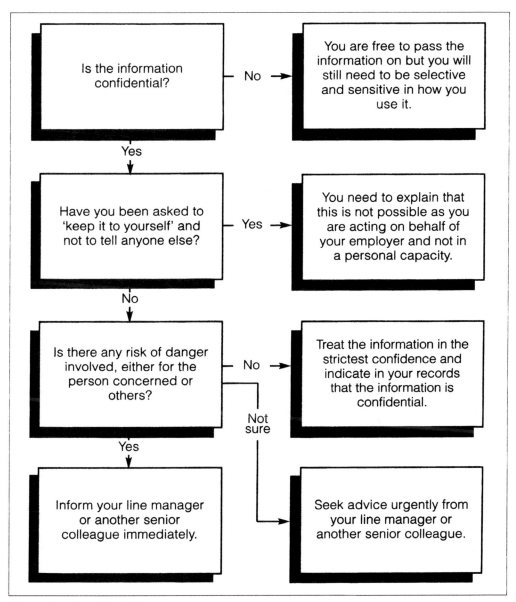

Figure 2.1   Confidentiality

Who should have access to that information? The short answer is: as few people as is necessary. Sensitive information needs to be treated as such – that is, *sensitively*. So, information should not be shared with people who do not need to know, nor should it be left in public areas. It is also important that all staff should be aware of confidentiality, including volunteers, domestic staff and so on.

Are there circumstances when different rules of access should apply? In situations such as when complaints are being investigated, police enquiries are being undertaken or court cases in progress, normal rules of access can be overruled. These are exceptional circumstances and you should be informed by your line manager about your obligations. There might well be new faces around at such times, which can be confusing, but do not work on assumptions about people's right to access. Never allow access to records, or proffer information, unless you are absolutely sure of the credentials of the person asking. Bona fide personnel will not mind you checking first.

How is information kept confidential? If records are kept manually, then confidentiality will not be maintained unless they are physically locked away somewhere. It is not enough to keep files in an unlocked cabinet in an office, for example. Unauthorised people would then only have to gain access to one room to be able to access material that should be confidential. It is very tempting to leave files on office desks while dealing with a matter that crops up unexpectedly, but confidentiality can so easily be breached in such circumstances, especially if the office is near to public access routes. Computerised records may seem, on the face of it, more secure, but unless there is a way of barring access, such as a password system, then information can be accessed fairly easily by unauthorised people, especially if records are stored and retrievable by name rather than being anonymised in some way.

Each organisation will have its own method of ensuring confidentiality and the need to comply with legal requirements regarding the storage of information. It is important that you make sure you play your part in ensuring that private information remains private unless there are extenuating circumstances. If you value the right to confidentiality then it is likely to remain high in your consciousness throughout the course of your daily work anyway, but make it your business to read policy guidelines and incorporate that guidance into your own practice. Taking responsibility as an individual worker is a good first step, but you will also need to play your part in ensuring that you are not the only person who takes these matters seriously. For example, do colleagues and those for whom you hold line management responsibility subscribe to these values and practices? Do they follow good practice guidelines because they understand them, or do they just see them as rules for the sake of rules? You are well placed to play a part in the process of fostering a culture of respect for confidentiality and it is something that is expected of you at this level, as we see below.

Exercise 2.7

Obtain a copy of your employer's policy on confidentiality. If there isn't one, then ask a manager to go over the main points with you. Consider whether the existing guidelines offer enough guidance for the situations you have encountered this far. Do you have a designated person to contact if you find yourself facing a dilemma that you can't resolve?

Maintaining the right ethos

However rigorously we maintain confidentiality in our practice, we cannot take responsibility for the practice of others. What we can do, though, is encourage a culture of confidentiality, making a respect for service users' rights in this area part of the value base of the *organisation*, as well as our own. One way of encouraging such an ethos is to raise awareness of obligations regarding confidentiality with new recruits at induction. An explicit written statement of values can make this task easier than just talking about it in a vague way. If no written statement of values exists you might want to look into developing such a statement. However, the mere fact of subscribing to a confidentiality clause or statement is not enough in itself. What is important is that staff not only maintain confidentiality but understand *why* they should. The requirement at this level for you to be involved in developing and evaluating methods and systems means that you have to think further than your own practice and your own value base and to that of those who work with and for you.

Working in partnership

We talked earlier about situations when it is appropriate or necessary to break a confidence, or refuse to be bound by confidentiality. Such decisions are not usually taken lightly, and if the right to confidentiality is breached, it is often because it is deemed to be in the service user's best interests. However, the service user is not inside your head with you and will be unaware of these thought processes unless you share them. A decision to break a confidence might well be perceived as a betrayal of trust by someone in your care who has not been able to appreciate the dilemmas you have faced in coming to that decision.

If you are open in your dealings with service users and make it clear at the outset of a relationship that you have obligations other than maintaining confidentiality at all costs, then the service user is less likely to feel betrayed and personalise the issue against you. Refusing to keep something confidential might make you unpopular in the short term, but you will keep your integrity intact in the long term.

2.6 Systems and structures

Earlier in this chapter, we described how discrimination operates at three different levels: personal, cultural and structural. One of the implications of this is that problems of discrimination can arise irrespective of individuals' intentions or wishes. Taken-for-granted assumptions, unwritten rules and other aspects of the cultural level can easily lead to discrimination, as we have seen. The way power works at a structural level can also lead to discrimination by reinforcing existing inequalities. Tackling inequality and affirming diversity therefore have to be seen as going beyond the actions of individuals. This is why systems and structures in organisations can be so important.

If there are no systems and structures in place to promote equality and affirm diversity, or what are in place are less than adequate, then we should not be surprised to find that discrimination and disadvantage continue to be significant problems. We are therefore faced with the challenge of trying to make sure that there are appropriate systems in place and that they function as they are intended.

You may be familiar with the saying, 'Think global, act local'. This refers to getting the 'big picture', seeing how things interrelate at the broader level (what is often referred to as the 'macro' level), while being able to intervene at the 'micro' level – those areas of your work over which you have control and influence. This is a good way of looking at the question of systems and structures. As an individual you cannot be held responsible for the organisation's overall systems and structures. You can, however, play a part in seeking to influence the organisation in whatever reasonable ways you can (see the discussion of the 'organisational operator' in Thompson, 2003b) and by playing at least a small part in dealing with matters at the level of policies and systems.

Important questions to address include the following:

- Do existing systems reflect equality and diversity? For example, does the allocation of work tasks avoid gender stereotyping?

- What systems and policies currently exist to promote equality and affirm diversity? For example, is there an equal opportunities policy, a diversity policy or other such formal approach to the issues?

- If such policies exist, are they actually implemented (or implemented appropriately)? A policy that exists on paper but has no actual bearing on what happens in reality can often be more of a hindrance than a help. It is important that policies are *operationalised* – that is, translated into reality.

- Are there any gaps in the existing systems and policies? Are there any important aspects of equality and diversity that are not covered in the existing set up?

Again it has to be emphasised that no one is trying to make you feel that you are personally responsible for the whole organisation, its systems and structures, but we all have a part to play. In a very real sense, the staff *are* the organisation.

2.7 Conclusion

As we have seen, the value base of social care is a very complex area. We have to recognise that we will need to continue to wrestle with the complexities for as long as we practise, rather than simply come up with a formula solution that provides simple answers or straightforward rules to follow.

Values are an important part of social care practice because they influence not only *what* we do (our decisions and actions) but also *how* we do it (our attitudes and approaches) and *why* we do it (our motivation). The time and effort required to wrestle with these complex issues is therefore a good investment, as we have so much to gain from having a clear picture of what our values are and how they affect us.

It is also important to recognise that failing to address values issues openly, directly and explicitly may mean that we unwittingly act against the interests of the service users we are endeavouring to support. Values, although difficult and slippery, none the less need to be kept in the forefront. Whatever we do in social care, wherever we operate, values will never be far away. It is therefore essential that we are clear about what our values are and how we intend to uphold them so that our actions are true to them. While much of what you are required to reflect on or demonstrate may seem, on the surface, to focus on what you should be doing, the *why* as well as the *what* is fundamental, and you will need to be able to demonstrate an understanding of this as part of your overall competence.

Chapter 3

Working in Partnership

3.1 Introduction

What is partnership?

What do we think of when we see the word partner? In conventional usage, it tends to suggest being one half of a twosome – perhaps in a social, sporting or business relationship. The following definition refers to a partner as: 'one that shares in the possession or enjoyment of something with another' (*Encyclopaedia Britannica*, p. 1648).

We would suggest that the concept of partnership can be widened to encompass more than just two people in a working relationship. Indeed, the actual number of participants is secondary to the more crucial aspect, that of sharing. It is this notion of sharing that will be the focus of this chapter. Working in partnership means exactly that – a sharing of the processes involved in social interaction, right through from the beginning stage when a problem is identified or an agenda raised, through joint investment in an agreed plan of action towards an end that has been jointly agreed as desirable. For the purposes of this chapter, then, partnership is about a sharing of responsibility – a sense of working with someone towards an end, rather than imposing change from without. Because social care work is 'people work' the relationship between people will always be a factor. As such, then, the discussion that follows will have significance for all four of the S/NVQ4 core units and, of course, for all of those which relate to people working with people. Indeed, because it relates to dignity and respect, it is likely to be one of the underpinning themes of any course of study relating to social care.

Exercise 3.1

Before moving on to look in more detail at what partnership entails, you may find it useful to consider the following questions:

- Can you think of any examples, in either your personal life or a work situation, where change has been imposed without your being involved in the negotiations?
- Who was involved in the process?
- How did this make you feel?
- What does this tell you about the value of working in partnership?

Partnership with whom?

What may have become evident from the previous exercise is that working in partnership, entailing as it does a sharing of responsibility, can involve a number of different people. In the field of social care, there may be several people, all of whom feel they have an interest in the health and well-being of the service user with whom you are working. For example, there may be a variety of professionals involved: health visitors, dieticians, teachers, doctors and social workers, to name but a few. Multidisciplinary working has much to commend it, as it provides an arena for sharing responsibility and for allowing workers and service users to benefit from the viewpoint and expertise of people from other disciplines. However, its success relies on effective communication and a willingness to consider other people's points of view, even when they may differ from your own. Multidisciplinary collaboration will be discussed in more detail in Section 3.

In the field of social care you are likely to be working with colleagues, rather than on your own, and even where you are a key worker, there will be other workers who share the care or supporting of a particular service user – that is, unless you are prepared to work 24 hours a day, 365 days a year! In such situations, progress is likely to be ineffective if people are pulling in different directions.

You may often be working alongside relatives and carers, within or outside a family setting. You may have become involved at the request of a service user or carer, or other professional. Either way, you may be able to benefit from being able to maintain a certain degree of emotional distance from what might be a tense family or group situation, because you are independent of that situation. However, it is often the case that service users, carers and concerned relatives, looking for 'the right answer' may look to you to provide that answer – to tell them what to do. It is important that the concept of partnership, with its emphasis on *sharing* responsibility for action planning towards shared goals, is not undermined by assumptions on either side, that it is someone else's responsibility. This will be discussed further in the following section.

One person who is often overlooked when discussing shared responsibility is the service user him – or herself. Rather than being at the centre of negotiations, there can be a tendency for the service user to be the last to be consulted about their views, if indeed at all. This is often the case with children or vulnerable adults who may have communication difficulties or lack the skills or confidence or, indeed, the opportunities to ensure that their voices are heard. Despite the challenge from the user involvement movement, elements of a paternalistic attitude (which maintains that children and vulnerable adults should defer to 'those who know best') still exist. Working in partnership has the potential to challenge this paternalistic ethos, but only if the service user is able to play a central role in decisions about his or her future.

Why is it important?

We have already alluded to some of the benefits to be gained from working in partnership. In this section we will make these points more explicitly. Before doing so, it would be useful to remind ourselves about the value base of social care work, as discussed in Chapter 2, and Exercise 3.2 is designed to help with this.

Exercise 3.2

Consider the following questions:
- Which aspects of your work give you most satisfaction?
- Do you sometimes feel 'uncomfortable' about any aspects of the work you are required to undertake?

This exercise will, we hope, have helped you to identify those values that you hold dear and would endeavour to promote in your work, and those which you think are inappropriate or damaging.

The success of the partnership approach relies on it being accepted as a core value. That is to say, it has to be accepted that service users have a right to be involved in joint decision making, or at the very least to have their opinions heard. If that premise is taken on board, and partnership practice is incorporated into our way of working, we would suggest that the following benefits would ensue. We would argue in favour of promoting partnership as a core practice for the following reasons:

- It promotes an ethos of empowerment. That is, by encouraging service users to contribute to, and share in the responsibility that ensues from, joint planning and decision making, service users are empowered, in the sense that they have the opportunity to develop new insight and skills which they can deploy in other situations. For example, it may give a service user the confidence to do his or her own negotiating in some future scenario, rather than having to rely on a professional 'problem solver'.

- By doing this, it also helps to create an ethos of *inter*dependency, rather than one of dependency, where the service user feels unable to reciprocate. This is often the case with older or disabled people, particularly those in residential care, who may feel that everything is being done to them, albeit with the best of intentions. Working in partnership with a service user provides opportunities for that service user to feel that he or she has something to give, as well as take, from the relationship, thereby discouraging dependency.

- It promotes service users' rights, such as the right to privacy, respect, confidentiality and so on, by providing the opportunity for service users to have their say in a working relationship where their input is encouraged and valued.

- It promotes effective change. Research, especially that in the management field, suggests that change is least effective when it is imposed from without, that is, introduced without prior consultation or discussion with the people most likely to be affected (see Hughes, 2006). It has been shown to be more readily accepted when those involved feel included in the process, with some understanding of the rationale behind the change and of the implications. If we take these research findings on board, then it suggests that there is more likelihood of a service user co-operating with plans aimed at changing, for example, an outlook, attitude or behaviour, if he or she feels part of the process and has an understanding of the rationale behind the proposals. Change can be very stressful, but if a service user accepts the 'ownership' of his or her problem, then commitment to seeing a potentially difficult process through to a conclusion is likely to be higher than it might otherwise have been.

- It helps to further weaken the ethos of paternalism which used to be a strong feature of social care earlier in the last century, when social problems tended to be seen as the result of personal inadequacy, and it was accepted that people experiencing problems should defer to 'those who know best'. Whilst such approaches have been strongly challenged by the development of the notion of empowerment (Neil Thompson, 2006d), there is still a tendency for some groups of vulnerable people to be disempowered by such thinking. Partnership practice recognises the power imbalance between service users and workers and tries to break down that barrier by promoting shared responsibility, with each partner having something to offer towards an end that has been agreed as desirable by the parties involved.

- It provides a challenge to the 'professional mystique' that some workers use to maintain their positions of power. By the use, for example of jargon or specialist terminology, or by speaking 'over someone's head' to a colleague, they are setting themselves apart from, and superior to, service users, and sometimes to colleagues from other disciplines. Working in partnership provides the opportunity for such practice to be challenged by encouraging service users to feel comfortable enough to be able to contribute, rather than by alienating or even frightening them by the abuse of power.

How do we achieve it?

Before discussing ways in which working in partnership can be integrated into daily working practices it is important to establish that a commitment to accepting it as a core value – rather than as an 'added extra' to be considered in an already pressurised job – is vital if it is to be successfully incorporated. Without this respect for service users' opinions and the commitment, throughout an organisation, to the principle of including clients in decisions which will affect their lives, partnership will be very difficult to achieve. Having this commitment written up as a mission statement or policy can provide a basis on which to build a team or organisational ethos rather than relying on the good practice, or otherwise, of individual workers.

Other important elements needed to promote partnership include:

- *Clarity* – be clear about what you are trying to achieve. We have already talked about how people are more accepting of change if they feel involved in the planning and execution of that change, but they are unlikely to have any strong commitment to it unless there are advantages to be gained from becoming involved in the change process, which can often be difficult or even traumatic. It is important, then, that goals and outcomes, and the means of achieving them, are clearly identified and recorded. If both worker and service user agree that an outcome is both desirable and achievable, then there is likely to be more chance of success than if matters just 'drift on', without any particular plan of action, or with one that has been decided on unilaterally (see the discussion below of 'systematic practice').

- *Empowerment* – make efforts to ensure that the service user feels able to participate. For example, he or she may feel disempowered by the following barriers to effective partnership:
  - communication difficulties, including the lack of a shared language, hearing loss, speech impairment;
  - a learning disability;
  - shyness or lack of confidence;
  - fear;
  - lack of awareness of the right to participate.

- *Role awareness* – if a service user is to work closely with a worker, sharing in the ownership of problems and solutions, then he or she needs to feel comfortable in that role. Part of the skill of working in partnership, then, is to be aware of how the service user perceives his or her role, and the balance of power between service user and worker, so that a comfortable relationship can be established wherever possible.

Exercise 3.3
Think carefully about how working together is, or could be, facilitated in your own workplace. What strengths can you build on? What areas for improvement exist?

In your responses to Exercise 3.3, you may have included the following:

- Providing facilities for people to communicate in the medium in which they feel most confident, including, for example, British Sign Language.

- Holding discussions in a situation where the service user does not feel overawed – perhaps in his or her own room, or on 'neutral territory', rather than in a manager's office.

- Ensuring that a chosen venue is accessible to all, including wheelchair users.

- The use of advocates, where a service user has difficulty in understanding procedures or communicating his or her needs.

- The use of techniques such as assertiveness training in order to empower people by boosting confidence, self-esteem and verbal and negotiating skills.

- Spreading the word – in the field of social care it is unlikely that you will be the only person working with a particular service user. For example, it is possible that teachers, health visitors, social workers, therapists, community nurses and any number of people from other disciplines may be involved, each having their own particular agenda with the service user, and each bringing their own personal and professional values to the situation. If working in partnership can be promoted across professional boundaries, as a core value, then joint working is likely to be more effective and less confusing and disempowering for the service user. We will look at multidisciplinary working in more detail in Section 3.3.

- Providing opportunities for wider involvement – working in partnership need not be restricted to one-to-one situations, or to a specific outcome. For example, service users could be invited to participate in workshops, planning meetings, training forums and so on. In this way, they can represent others in similar, or potentially similar situations to their own, and contribute towards ensuring that users' perspectives are heard at all stages of planning and implementation of services and facilities. This enables service users' strengths to be utilised, and may result in resources being targeted into projects that are more likely to meet their needs.

- Examining our own attitudes – working in partnership is likely to be no more than a paper exercise if we do not take every opportunity to accord service users the dignity and respect that is their right as individuals, regardless of age, class, ethnicity, gender, sexual orientation or whatever. Unless we are totally committed to the partnership philosophy, we may be giving out signals that disempower people by making them feel inferior. For example, do we always ask service users how they would like to be addressed? Do we always respect their personal space? Are we always sensitive to how a female service user may perceive a male worker and vice versa, and how either party can feel threatened by the other? Unless we give out messages that we respect service users' participation, then it is unlikely that the ethos of trust necessary for effective practice will develop.

- Respecting confidentiality – in order for a service user to feel comfortable in the role of 'sharing' the solution to a problem, or the response to an identified need, he or she needs to feel sure that the relationship is based on mutual respect. This can be maintained by being careful about who you share information with and why. Working in a multidisciplinary setting, or in situations where lots of workers are involved, increases the potential for information to be widely disseminated. It is often the case that it is necessary for that information to be shared, in the interest of the service user, and in such cases he or she needs to be aware that such information will be shared. It is damaging to the relationship of trust if a service user is promised that information will remain 'our secret', when, because of statutory obligations, for example, it may have to be disclosed to others. Clarity and honesty about what cannot be kept confidential is therefore very important at the outset of any joint work. In any other situation, thought should be given to who, if anyone, needs to have access to information about plans of action that have been jointly agreed by a worker and service user and how it can be ensured that only those who need it have access to information about him or her. This may be, for example, a residential worker on a different shift, a relief worker or a line manager.

Exercise 3.4

Consider the following questions relating to how information is recorded in your work situation:

- Who has access to it?
- Has the service user given permission for that information to be shared?
- How might you feel if you discovered that information you disclosed to your doctor, for example, had been passed to your dentist, without your permission?
- Can you see parallels in the situation your service users might be in?

Clearly, then, there are a number of steps that can be taken to help make partnership a reality, rather than just a fashionable 'buzzword'. Important themes that emerge from this include the role of negotiation, trust and the need to see positive gains from the active involvement of service users.

3.2 Relationships with service users

Introduction

It could be argued that good relationships with service users are a fundamental part of social care. To be effective workers we need to *engage* with people – that is, to build up a rapport and establish a working relationship where both parties feel at least reasonably comfortable with one another. How can we be expected to achieve anything if we do not have the sound foundation of a good relationship to build on? Clearly, service user relationships are very important indeed. However, as we shall be arguing here, the situation with regard to relationships is not as simple and straightforward as is generally believed.

This part of the chapter explores what is involved in building and sustaining effective working relationships with service users. The first section addresses questions relating to the skills involved, the *interpersonal* skills we need to carry out our work to the high standard that users of social care services deserve. And, of course, social care is a very skilled job – it is not just a matter of using our personality or natural abilities.

The second section is concerned with systematic practice, an important element of effective working relationships with service users. It explains the important role of keeping a clear focus on the purpose of our work so that the basis of the professional relationship is not distorted. By exploring the notion of 'systematic practice', we are also laying the foundations for a more detailed consideration of systematic practice as the basis of assessment (see Chapter 4).

Interpersonal skills

A basic part of good practice in social care is what is commonly known as 'use of self'. This means being able to draw on our own life experiences and our own personality to help others. It also means being able to relate to other people on a 'person to person' basis, allowing them to see us as real people, as individuals in our own right and also allowing us to see them as unique individuals with a life-story or 'biography' of their own.

While some people may see 'use of self' as simply a natural ability that some people have but others do not. This is an oversimplification. It fails to recognise:

1. Just how much skill is involved in effective use of self; and
2. That skills, even complex interpersonal skills, can be learned.

We therefore have to be careful about underestimating how much is involved in effective interpersonal interactions, and how great the scope is for developing our existing skills and learning new ones. While we may all have some degree of ability in relating to other people (it is, after all a basic part of being a member of society), there are surely none of us who can realistically claim that we have nothing further to learn, no further improvements to work on. Our aim here, then, is not to 'start from scratch', but rather, to accept that everyone has some degree of skill and to work towards enhancing and consolidating those skills as far as possible.

Before looking at some of the specific skills involved, have a look at Exercise 3.5, as this is designed to help you get an overview of the various elements involved in interpersonal skills.

Exercise 3.5

Spend a few moments considering what is involved in developing and maintaining effective working relationships with service users. What skills would you include? Which of these are you good at? Are there any you struggle with? What areas of skill would you like to improve if you could? Feel free to undertake this exercise with a colleague or friend if you would find this helpful.

Communicating effectively

Communication is generally recognised as an important part of effective relationships – if we do not communicate very effectively, how can we keep a relationship going? It is therefore important to be clear about what is involved in effective communication. For present purposes, we can break this down into two main parts: getting your message across ('transmission') and listening to other people's points of view ('reception').

(i) Getting your message across

How do we communicate effectively? How do we succeed in getting our message across? These are important questions and deserve close attention.

There are four chapters in *People Skills* that are concerned in some way with the process of getting our message across. These are as follows:

- Chapter 10 addresses verbal forms of communication and explores the various factors that can help or hinder us in trying to express ourselves clearly and effectively. This chapter summarises many of the key issues involved.

- Chapter 11 concentrates on non-verbal communication, the subtle workings of body language that can be so influential in shaping how people respond to each other. This chapter tries to help readers build on their existing skills in using and reading body language by developing a greater sensitivity and awareness of the complex meanings associated with non-verbal forms of communication.

- Chapter 12 is concerned with written forms of communication, and these too are important elements of being able to get our message across. Social care workers are frequently required to communicate in writing, for example in letters or reports, and so the skills involved in this are important ones to develop, even though this may prove difficult for some staff who have memories of negative experiences of written communication dating back to their schooldays.

- Chapter 13 focuses on interviewing as an important set of social care skills. This involves, for example, getting the time and the place right – the broader issues that can get in the way of effective communication if we are not sufficiently 'tuned in' to them.

Of course, these four chapters will not provide you with all you need in terms of understanding the complexities of communication, but they should provide you with a foundation on which to build future learning and skill development. For an equally accessible but more in-depth discussion of the importance of communication, see Neil Thompson's book, *Communication and Language: A Handbook of Theory and Practice* (Thompson, 2003a).

Exercise 3.6

Read the above four chapters from *People Skills* and make notes on what you see as the main points.

(ii) Listening

Listening is, of course, more than simply using our ears in a straightforward way. It implies also making the effort to take on board what is being said to us, paying attention to what is being conveyed to us by the other person or persons. Listening involves:

- *Acknowledging that we are listening* – reassuring the other person that we are paying attention (for example, through eye contact or nodding). This is part of what is known as 'active' listening.

- *Being patient* – This involves three main elements: i) taking turns – giving people the space to talk, without interrupting them; ii) tolerating silences where appropriate (avoiding the temptation to remove any tension by 'filling' the gaps); and iii) not jumping to conclusions by, for example, relying on stereotypes or other prejudicial assumptions.

- *'Reading' body language* – Often a person's non-verbal communication will tell us a great deal about their emotional state or about the message they are trying to convey. If we are not paying attention to what the body language is telling us, then we are not really listening.

- *Reflection and summary* – It can be very helpful to reflect back to people what you understand them to be saying to you, perhaps by summarising your understanding of what they have said. This can help to identify potential or actual misunderstandings and is also a good way of reassuring the other person that we have indeed been listening.

- *Having time* – Listening takes time. It is no good saying that we feel listening is an essential skill in social care and then not leaving ourselves enough time to do it properly. Effective listening therefore owes something to good time management skills (see Chapter 6).

Building trust

Getting our message across clearly and listening well are both important parts of building trust. However, there are also other important steps we can take to help build trust – and it is important that we recognise and work on these, as a lack of trust tends to be a major obstacle to effective working relationships.

What else, then, is involved in building trust? We would argue that the following issues, although not forming an exhaustive list, are fundamental aspects of building a foundation of trust from which good working relationships can be developed:

- *Honesty and openness* – This means having a shared agenda, rather than one person making decisions behind the other's back. Important issues should be shared, with no holding back of significant information. If someone is given only half the story, he or she is unlikely to feel comfortable and willing to trust. This also involves being prepared to admit mistakes.

- *Recognising our limitations* – There are limits to what we can offer and to what we can achieve, and so there is little point refusing to acknowledge our limitations. Clarity about what we can and cannot do is a helpful part of building relationships based on trust. No one will respect us for being unrealistic about our capabilities, with insufficient awareness of our limitations.

- *Reliability* – There is no substitute for reliability, even though no one is perhaps one hundred per cent reliable. We should, however, make sure that, as far as possible, we turn up when we are expected to, do what we have agreed to and refrain from doing what we have agreed not to – or communicating why it has not been possible to do this if circumstances beyond our control have intervened.

- *Working in partnership* – The whole theme of partnership is geared towards building and maintaining relationships premised on trust and clear mutual expectations. In this respect, all the steps we take towards achieving social care based on partnership can be seen as steps geared towards building trust.

Handling aggression

Chapters 5 and 16 of *People Skills* discuss much of what is involved in dealing with conflict and aggression. Chapter 5 concentrates on assertiveness and considers how and why we should seek to establish a positive balance between the two extremes of an aggressive approach and one that is submissive. Such assertiveness skills can be very useful in defusing or preventing conflict situations and thus sidestepping the potential for aggression and violence.

In some ways, Chapter 16 builds on this by exploring what can be done in situations where conflict has begun to arise or where aggression is a possible, likely or actual outcome. The key theme here is that of negotiation, the set of skills that equip us to handle conflicts positively and constructively as far as possible.

Exercise 3.7

You should now read Chapters 5 and 16 of *People Skills* and answer the questions below. Once again, it is not a case of finding the 'right answers', but rather an opportunity for exploring the issues and developing your understanding of them. Feel free to discuss your ideas with a colleague or friend.

1. What aspects of assertiveness do you feel you are good at? Are there any areas where you feel you could improve?
2. How well developed are your negotiation skills? Which aspects of negotiation do you find most difficult? Is there anything you could do to develop your skills in this area?

Handling feelings

We referred earlier to the need to engage with the people with whom we work and this leads on to another important aspect of interpersonal communication, that is, the question of handling feelings – other people's and your own. It is worth considering each of these two aspects separately.

- *Other people's feelings*: It is important that we are able to 'read' other people's feelings, and the ability to interpret non-verbal communication can therefore be seen as an essential part of being sensitive to people's feelings. Being able to detect particular body language 'signals' or to recognise the significance of differences in tone of voice are important communication skills. But there is more to it than this. We also have to be able to 'put ourselves in the other person's shoes', to try and appreciate how they are likely to be feeling in their particular situation (Sue Thompson, 2002). But, this is not to say that it is wise to make comments like 'I know how you feel'. We do *not* know how someone else feels, and it can be very intrusive for us to tell someone that we do. We may know how we would feel in their circumstances or we may have some fairly clear clues about their feelings, but this is not the same as 'knowing how you feel'. It is not uncommon for people to react very strongly to such comments, showing that, in effect, we are adding insult to injury by making such remarks.

- *Our own feelings*: Sometimes the idea that social care staff should be 'professional' in their dealings with service users is misinterpreted. It is mistakenly seen as an expectation that staff should not have any emotional responses to the situations they encounter as part of their work. Clearly, it is unrealistic to expect an emotionally neutral approach to care work, and a more helpful attitude is one in which we recognise the important part our own feelings play and consider how best to deal with them. This can be seen to involve:
  - recognising when our feelings are influencing our actions (for example, if we are angry towards someone);
  - understanding how our feelings interact with, and influence, the feelings of others (which is partly why feelings are an important aspect of interpersonal relationships);
  - using our feelings positively as a means of forming and sustaining effective relationships (open expression of our own feelings encourages others to express their feelings).

If we do not pay attention to the skills involved in handling feelings, there is a danger that we will contribute to a situation where people feel it is not safe, appropriate or helpful to talk about their feelings. We can therefore unwittingly help to create an atmosphere in which the expression of feelings is hindered rather than helped – a potentially very harmful situation for most, if not all, of the people who receive social care services.

Systematic practice

The basic idea underpinning systematic practice is that, at all times, we should be clear about what we are doing and why we are doing it. This is something we shall look into in more detail in Chapter 4 when we consider what is involved in assessment. Although this principle sounds simple and straightforward, trying to put it into practice in a busy, pressurised work environment, with lots of competing demands on our time, can be very difficult at times. It has to be recognised that systematic practice is a skilled activity that can take a long time to develop. It is not simply a matter of applying a principle in a routine or mechanical way.

What service users want

Over the years there has been a great deal of 'consumer' research investigating what people want or expect from social work and social care, and how satisfied they have been in relation to what they have received. A recurring theme throughout these studies has been the importance of clarity about what the worker is doing – about what he or she is working towards, how and why. This is entirely consistent with systematic practice, in the sense that the underlying principle is one of clarity about purpose, with an honest and open approach to working towards achieving agreed ends.

Keeping a clear focus

The basis of systematic practice is the ability to keep a clear focus on what is happening in terms of what we are trying to achieve, on the *purpose* of our work with this particular individual, family or group. This involves avoiding *drift*, the tendency to lose track of what we are doing and why we are doing it.

Drift is a phenomenon that often occurs when people are busy, with a lot of different tasks and pressures to deal with at the same time. We can get so engrossed in what we are doing that we lose our focus on what it is that we are actually trying to do – what goals we are working towards. This is something that applies not only in social care but also in life more generally. It is a process that we are all prone to, at certain times at least. However, it is one that we have to guard against, as drift stands in the way of good practice in general and partnership in particular.

Staying professional

Forming effective working relationships can be summed up as 'being friendly without being friends'. There has to be a good relationship based on trust, respect and professional credibility. Service users must be able to feel that they are valued and their concerns are taken seriously by someone who can be relied upon to work constructively with them. At times, this can amount to getting very close to the person concerned. However, we need to recognise that the relationship must none the less remain a professional one.

There are a number of reasons for this, not least the following:

- *Jealousy*: Going beyond a professional relationship with one service user can cause jealousy, resentment and ill-feeling among other service users (or even among colleagues).

- *Personal space*: An important part of stress management is the ability to gain a degree of respite from work pressures, to draw a boundary around them so that we can cut ourselves off from them when we need to. Where relationships go beyond the professional, we may have difficulty in drawing such boundaries and maintaining the personal space we need to keep pressures at manageable levels. This extends beyond a personal responsibility and so, if you have line management responsibilities and the health and safety obligations that go along with them, there is the threat that stress can pose to employees' and colleagues' mental health to consider too.

- *Moving on*: No one is obliged to remain in the same job forever, and movement of staff from job to job is a very common phenomenon. This can be very problematic if relationships have developed to the extent where the departure of a member of staff leads to a fairly traumatic experience for one or more service users. Some degree of sadness at a member of staff moving on is to be expected and is not necessarily a problem. However, this can be taken to harmful extremes at times.

- *Drift*: As outlined above, drift can be a significant problem, as busy staff lose the focus of what they are doing and why they are doing it. Sometimes the nature of the relationship between staff member and service user can contribute to drift. That is, the further away from a professional relationship we move, the greater is the likelihood that we will lose our focus on the professional task.

- *Dependency*: One of the dangers involved in social care is that we can, often unwittingly, make people dependent upon us. That is, they can come to rely on us to meet certain needs or solve certain problems, rather than use what we offer to learn how to do this for themselves as part of a process of empowerment. Some types of relationship in social care can therefore be inappropriate because they encourage dependency rather than empowerment.

Exercise 3.8

The question of relationships and what constitutes an appropriate professional relationship is a very complex one, and one where there are different views as to what is or is not good practice. For this exercise, you are therefore asked to consider your own views on relationships and identify what you see as the key factors, the important issues that help you decide what is appropriate in a relationship with a service user and what is not. Where would you draw the line and why? You may find it helpful to discuss these issues with one or more colleagues.

3.3 Multidisciplinary collaboration

Understanding roles

First of all, what do we mean by a role? When we interact with other people, we do not always present ourselves, or are not perceived by others, in the same way. There are different expectations on us according to the role we are playing at the time. For example, we can play the role of parent, sibling, teacher, housekeeper, student, care worker and probably many other roles at one and the same time, each role incorporating a set of expectations, based on people's perception of those roles.

There are differing theories about how those expectations have arisen, some of which seek to explain why they differ between cultures and over time. Goffman (1959), for example, suggests that we are socialised into learning 'scripts' that are appropriate for the different roles we have to play in life, in the same way that professional actors do when performing a drama. There is a tendency for people to have preconceived ideas about what type of behaviour we expect from, for example, a barrister in a courtroom scene or a doctor in a surgery, and are often surprised if one of them acts atypically. This is because we have expectations of that role which we have built up over time. It must be remembered, however, that these expectations are culturally specific. For example, a person visiting a doctor's surgery in a culture where sickness is believed to be caused by evil spirits might have expectations of the doctor that require that he or she will perform dances to exorcise demons. Such a response would not be seen as appropriate in a culture where there is an expectation that the doctor will examine the patient in a methodical, scientific manner, test for chemical imbalances and administer medication.

It is precisely because roles, and the expectations they engender, are not fixed that we need to be sensitive to how others perceive us, and how we perceive other people. If we rely on fixed, stereotypical definitions of what a role 'should' involve, then we are relying on someone else's value judgement, rather than basing our expectations on our own inquiry and values. We will look at stereotyping and its potentially harmful effects later in the section.

Exercise 3.9

Take this opportunity to reflect on the roles you are required to play, and the expectations they place on you. Consider the expectations placed on you in your present job. Try to identify the different roles you play during a typical working day. Do these roles overlap? Do they produce conflicting expectations?

It will probably have become clear, following Exercise 3.9, that we each play many different roles at different times, and that unless other people understand what obligations each particular role involves, a great deal of confusion and disappointment is likely to ensue. In the field of social care, there is the potential for such a lack of clarity to lead to a blurring of the distinction between roles, especially when people are working to broadly similar ends – a social worker and a community psychiatric nurse working to maintain an older service user with dementia in the community, perhaps. We have talked already about the need for clarity, and it is especially important here. If we are not clear about the obligations our own role places on us, or base our expectations of others on assumptions about their roles, rather than on knowledge, then there is the potential for obligations to service users to be forgotten about, or ignored on the false assumption that it is someone else's responsibility.

There are harmful consequences for workers too. Unreasonable or mistaken expectations of one's role can lead to high levels of stress, as we either try to live up to what is being demanded of us, or challenge other people's expectations of us. This can be described as role stress. Thompson *et al.* (1994) describe how this role stress can take different forms, as the following two examples illustrate:

- *Role ambiguity* – this arises when the boundaries are not made clear. It is often the case that we are the only person around at the time of an emergency or crisis, and we may be asked to take on roles that are beyond the scope of our training, experience or professional responsibility. Tackling the world's problems is outside the remit of most people's job, but there are times when we feel that it is being required of us. If we are aware of the boundaries of our own particular role, and are supported by our managers by not being required to overstep those boundaries, then we can work to the best of our abilities within those boundaries. Where there is ambiguity, particularly about what is not our responsibility, there is the potential for stress to build up (see Thompson *et al.*, 1996, for further discussion on the harmful effects of stress).

- *Role incompatibility* – we have already discussed how roles can conflict, and you may have been able to highlight experiences in your own situation. For example, a manager may see a worker, primarily, as a gatekeeper of scarce resources, while that worker may see him or herself as a service user's advocate for a share in those resources. Within families, too, there may be conflicting expectations of a worker's role. When becoming involved in family conflict a worker might be seen as an advocate by one member, and someone who is expected to be a figure of authority by another. Social care involves many such dilemmas, and tolerating a certain level of role incompatibility is part and parcel of the job. However, it must be recognised as a stressor, and steps taken to lessen its effect as far as possible. One way is to remain as focused as possible – to think carefully about what we are trying to achieve, what exactly our own role in that project is and to ensure that others are aware of where our responsibility begins and ends. As previously discussed, working in partnership requires a high degree of clarity about objectives, but it also requires that we communicate those objectives to others involved, so that all parties know what role the worker is taking on in a given situation. Communication skills will be discussed more fully in the final section.

Stereotypes

We have already identified a role as a set of expectations, but how do we build up those expectations of the behaviour and obligations of someone in any particular role? Exercise 3.10 is designed to help answer this question.

Exercise 3.10

Try to answer the following questions of a colleague of yours who is from a different discipline from your own. This will be a useful exercise if you are taking a foundation degree, because it will help both to broaden your understanding of the field and also to get you thinking about multidisciplinary collaboration and the potential it holds for good social care provision. And, if you are an S/NVQ4 candidate, you might also find it a useful start in terms of your obligations to demonstrate continuous professional development, and facilitate such in others.

- What is your understanding of his or her role?
- How did you acquire that information?
- Has there ever been any misunderstanding about what his or her responsibilities are?

What may have emerged from the above exercise is that we pick up information from a variety of sources within the culture in which we live and work – perhaps from personal experience, but also from anecdotes, jokes and images we see and hear in the media, where professional characteristics are often exaggerated or misrepresented. When we meet a person, we do not have time to recall and analyse all the information we have ever absorbed and incorporated into a set of expectations, and so we tend to rely on an image that typifies our expectations – a 'typification'. This might appear to be a useful short-cut but there is a danger that the process of typification can allow those representations to become fixed and inflexible – to become *stereotypes*. That is, it can be used to represent all people in a particular role and does not take into account diversity and individuality. By relying on caricatures and denying diversity, stereotypes tend to become vehicles for negative attitudes. For example:

- All women are weak and indecisive.
- All teenagers are rebellious.
- All older people lose their intellectual faculties.

If we do not constantly analyse the influences we see and hear, and become discerning of what we hear about other people, we run the risk of being influenced by negative stereotypes – of assuming that certain groups of people will necessarily have the characteristics that stereotypes imply. Since stereotyping tends to attach negative characteristics to certain groups of people, it can be seen to have a role in marginalising those groups and in maintaining power in the hands of those who have the means to promote those images. There is clearly a role for those who work in social care to challenge stereotyping wherever they encounter it, so that individuals, both colleagues and service users, are seen as unique people, with their own strengths and weaknesses, rather than as stereotypes.

How do we avoid stereotyping?

One important way is by being reflective in our own practice. Rather than following long-established practices and routines unthinkingly, we can think about whether those practices are oppressing service users by relying on stereotypical assumptions about what a person 'should be like'. For example, consider the following questions:

- Do we sometimes treat older people in a way that we would not treat a person who was thirty years younger, perhaps by preventing them from living 'at risk', because it is assumed that they are physically and intellectually frail, just by virtue of having been defined as 'old'?
- Do we sometimes not offer childcare and family support services to 'travelling' families because of the stereotypical assumption that 'they look after their own'?
- Do we sometimes assume that children do not grieve, and perhaps therefore offer counselling to their parents following a death or a critical incident, while under-estimating the child's distress?

- Do we sometimes assume that black people are more emotionally volatile than white people and base our assessment of their mental health on such a stereotype?

It is not easy to be self-critical, but if we are to challenge the destructive potential of stereotyping, it is necessary to heighten our self-awareness and to ensure that we are not playing a part in perpetuating the stereotypes that exclude certain groups of people from positions of power, and prevent service users from being seen as individuals with their own unique characteristics, rather than as 'one of them'.

Another important step forward is to challenge stereotyping in others. Oppressive humour is one example. Humour can play a part in relieving stress and making emotionally difficult jobs more bearable. If, however, the joke is at the expense of someone who is being demeaned by the perpetuation of a stereotype – for example, that Irish people are stupid, or black men are over-sexed and dangerous to women – then such humour is oppressive and to be challenged.

Non-accessibility of services is also an important issue. It is sometimes assumed by service providers that some ethnic minority communities do not require services – that they rely on each other rather than the state. If the situation were to be properly assessed, rather than assumptions based on stereotypes, then it might be the case that the need is actually there, but that services cannot be accessed because they are not being made accessible to non-English speakers.

In addition, the attitudes of colleagues from other fields may have to be challenged at times. If we have heightened our own self-awareness, we might be better able to recognise when others, with whom we work collaboratively, are potentially or actually oppressing service users because of stereotypical viewpoints, arising from either personal prejudice or differing practice ideologies.

As the discussion this far has emphasised, relying on stereotyping is not conducive to anti-oppressive practice. If working in partnership is to be the empowering project that is envisaged, then it is important that we do not work on assumptions about what, for example, nurses are like, but rather by getting to know what skills and knowledge a particular nurse colleague can bring to a situation. Likewise, our service users will be empowered if we see them as individuals from a particular culture, rather than as stereotypical clones. Stereotyping, then, is clearly a serious barrier to effective multidisciplinary collaboration.

Partnership skills

Understanding the principles of working in partnership is one thing, putting them into practice is perhaps another. There are skills involved, but most are unlikely to be new to you. You are probably already using them in your day-to-day work. Once you are committed to working in partnership with service users, it should just be a case of honing those skills and looking critically at the ways they can be applied, so that working with, rather than doing to, becomes the order of the day.

- *Communication* – We have already discussed the importance of communicating clearly and effectively. It is especially important in this respect, because working together means working towards the same end – a proposed outcome that has been jointly agreed upon. There is, therefore, no room for ambiguity. All parties need to be clear about what is to be achieved and how to go about achieving it. While verbal and written communication skills are important, attention also needs to be paid to listening effectively. If service users are to become partners in decision-making then we must learn to listen to what they are saying. Before moving on, we perhaps need to remind ourselves of the need to respect confidentiality when communicating with others, obtaining the service user's permission to share information unless there are extenuating circumstances, such as disclosure of child abuse, which override this principle.

- *Negotiation* – We have already identified negotiation as a key factor in working in partnership. Rather than change being imposed from without, options are discussed and a way forward is negotiated. See Chapter 16 of *People Skills* for a more detailed discussion of negotiating skills.

- *Assertiveness* – If we accept that the power relationship between worker and service user is an unequal one, biased in favour of the worker, it can be seen that the service user is likely to be disadvantaged when it comes to negotiating. Workers may have experience and training to draw upon, as well as the backing of an organisation, while it may be the first time a service user has been called on to participate in important decisions, or give their opinions on matters that are under discussion. Empowering service users with assertiveness skills can help to redress this imbalance of power, by boosting confidence and self-esteem, so that the right to participation is both recognised and acted upon. Workers, too, can often feel intimidated in the presence of colleagues. Being clear in your own mind about the boundaries of your own role can help boost your own confidence to challenge others who may have unreasonable expectations of you.

- *Being clear about boundaries* – This is not just about being clear about who does what, and ensuring that service users have access to whoever can best offer the expertise they require, but also about recognising boundaries of responsibility. Working in partnership requires that each party keeps his or her side of the bargain, but we can only be held responsible for what is within our sphere of control. That is, we cannot hold ourselves responsible for the failure of other people, or organisations, to 'come up with the goods'.

- *Unconditional positive regard* – If working in partnership requires us to build up relationships with our service users that are based on trust and integrity, what happens if we are required to work with someone we do not like, perhaps someone who has committed an offence, or lives a lifestyle of which we disapprove? Is it possible to work in partnership in such circumstances? The concept of unconditional positive regard addresses this issue. The term was coined by Rogers (1961) who refers to the need to have a non-judgemental attitude when involved in 'people work'. That is to say, we should not judge people against our own personal standards and values. When working in partnership, we should not be aiming to convert a person to our own moral viewpoint, but rather to work towards an outcome from which all parties will benefit. It is likely that workers in the field of social care will come across people they dislike, but we must not let this stand in the way of doing our best for those people, nor offer them a lesser service than any other service user might receive. We would wish to promote working in partnership as a core principle, rather than one to be practised or withheld according to our own preference. To suggest that our own views are 'superior' would not be conducive to a way of working that seeks to undermine working practices that are based on an 'I know best' attitude.

- *Using difference positively* – This means regarding differences between groups of people as a source of strength. Differences should be seen as an aspect of the richness of diversity, rather than as a set of problems or difficulties. Partnership is not about everyone trying to be the same, but rather taking the opportunity to learn from each other and benefit from our differences.

Clearly, partnership work is a skilled and demanding activity, and is not going to develop overnight. The skills described here (and others besides) take time to develop, and so a commitment to developing partnership is a long-term one, but none the less one that should repay the efforts involved in terms of the standards of practice to be achieved.

3.4 Conclusion

It is unfortunate that the term 'partnership' has come to be a fashionable one, as this means that it is often used uncritically, without its implications being considered. However, it is to be hoped that this chapter and the related readings will have helped to establish just how important a concept it is, and why it is necessary to take it seriously enough to devote the time and effort needed to make it a reality.

Partnership is clearly a complex notion, and one that takes a certain amount of time to develop as the basis of social care practice. We have come a long way since the early days of the social (care) worker being seen as a sort of 'social doctor' who diagnoses the problem and prescribes the treatment without necessarily taking on board the views of the person, family or group concerned. However, the more traditional, paternalistic approach has not died out altogether – it still shows its face from time to time, often in very subtle ways. The movement towards partnership-based approaches has therefore been consider-able, but we should not be complacent enough to think that we have achieved all that we need to.

Chapter 4

Understanding Assessment

4.1 Introduction

Assessment is a commonly used word in social care. However, it is also one of those words that is so widely used that it can easily be employed in an uncritical way, with a lack of clarity about what it means, what it involves or how it works. This chapter therefore seeks to explore a range of issues related to assessment in order to develop your understanding of this very important foundation of good practice in social care. Whatever you are doing in the social care field, and your study of it, there will be a focus on the skills involved in carrying out a specific task and on the underpinning knowledge and values. However, as with any task, there is no point trying to address something if you haven't established exactly what it is that needs addressing. And yet, all too often, people rush into the 'doing' stage without assessing what it is that he or she is trying to achieve by their intervention. This chapter, then, seeks to clarify:

- what is involved in assessment;
- how it fits into the broader social care process; and
- how it can go wrong.

We also focus later on one particular form of assessment, namely risk assessment. Risk is increasingly being recognised as an important factor in social care. However, it is also one that is often misunderstood and oversimplified. It is therefore important to look carefully at what is involved in the assessment of risk.

4.2 Assessing needs and circumstances

What is assessment?

Perhaps it would be helpful to start by being clear about what assessment is not in order to clear away some misconceptions, before tackling what is actually involved. Assessment is not:

- *Being judgemental* – What is being assessed is the *situation* overall, rather than a judgement being made about the service user as to whether or not he or she is deserving of help. Of course, he or she is part and parcel of the situation being assessed, but we should not adopt a narrow perspective that sees the individual but neglects the wider context.
- *Filling in forms* – Some assessment processes involve filling in forms, many including boxes to be ticked and so on. However, it should be noted that, while the form may

be completed as part of the process of assessment, it does not *constitute* the process of assessment. Assessment is much more than completing a form. Sometimes practitioners may say 'I have completed my assessment' when what they mean is that they have filled in the form. They confuse one aspect of the overall process with the process itself.

- *A search for 'right answers'* – Different people will assess situations in different ways. There is no one 'right answer' or ultimate truth that we are searching for when we undertake an assessment. This is not to say that 'anything goes' and that there are no wrong answers! The fact remains, however, that a degree of subjectivity is inevitable because the situation has to be interpreted – the facts do not speak for themselves. This is one of the important reasons why assessment should be carried out in partnership – so that other people have an input and therefore reduce the possibility of one individual's views being biased or distorted.

- *Diagnosis* – Traditional social care owes much to a medical model of practice. For example, many older texts use terms like diagnosis and treatment, rather than assessment and intervention. This is problematic in two ways: i) it assumes that the 'fault' lies with the individual and therefore tends to 'pathologise' the service user, placing him or her at the centre of the problem, rather than adopting a more holistic view that takes account of a wider range of factors; and ii) it sets the worker up as an 'expert', someone who is expected to have the answers (rather than someone who empowers people by facilitating and supporting them in finding their own answers).

Having clarified what assessment is *not*, it is now time to consider what is actually involved in undertaking an assessment. Exercise 4.1 is designed to help us do this.

Exercise 4.1

Chapter 19 of *People Skills* is devoted to the topic of assessment. Read that chapter now and consider the following questions.
1. How does assessment feature in your current workload? When are you called upon to assess situations?
2. Which aspects of assessment do you feel you are good at?
3. Which aspects would you like to improve on?

The helping process

Assessment is a fundamental part of what Neil Thompson refers to as the 'helping process' (2002a). The social work literature base provides examples of how the process (or set of processes) involved in carrying out this work is conceptualised in different ways by different authors (see Adams, 2002). The particular framework which follows, while not the only one, is widely used within social work but need not be confined to it, as it has a much broader application which includes social care work in general. It involves five stages as follows:

- *Assessment* – As we have seen, assessment is the beginning of the process, in so far as it involves developing a picture of the situation being dealt with, the needs and circumstances of the people involved, the problems and threats they face, as well as the strengths they can draw upon and the opportunities they may be able to exploit. Assessment also involves developing a plan of action, as clear a picture as possible of what needs to be done. This then acts as the basis of the remaining four stages.

- *Intervention* – Addressing unmet needs, tackling problematic circumstances, building on strengths, learning new skills, making new links – these are all steps that can come under the heading of intervention. How do we decide what steps to take? Well, that depends on our assessment, of course. If we are not clear what the problem is, we should not be surprised when we find it difficult to work out what the potential solutions are. Sound intervention therefore depends on sound assessment. This is also another reason why assessment needs to be undertaken in partnership. If service users have not been involved in deciding what is to be done, then there is a much higher chance that they will not feel committed to taking the necessary steps to tackle the problems identified – they will not 'own' the problem to the same extent, and are therefore much less likely to own any proposed solutions.

- *Review* – There are two main reasons why it is necessary to keep our work under review: (i) Situations change. What proves to be an excellent and very accurate assessment one day may prove to be inaccurate and out of date a day, week or month later. We therefore have to monitor the situation, rather than assume that our initial assessment continues to apply. Where it becomes apparent that changes have occurred, a review, formal or informal, is called for so that the assessment can be updated and amended as appropriate.
  (ii) We are not infallible! Even a very experienced, highly skilled worker can and will make mistakes, so we have to have the humility to recognise that our initial assessment needs to be reviewed from time to time to ensure, as far as possible, that we are able to identify any mistakes, omissions or oversights, and take the necessary steps to rectify them.

- *Ending or 'termination'* – Traditional social work practice was characterised by an open-ended approach, with a focus on extended casework (Payne, 2005). Consequently, the termination of intervention was not given as much attention as the other stages. Indeed, even today the termination of intervention is often neglected, despite the significance of effective and appropriate endings. Such appropriate termination will, of course, owe much to the assessment. Knowing when and how to bring a piece of work to a close will depend to a large extent on the nature and contents of the assessment and the needs, circumstances and so on identified at that stage and subsequently confirmed or amended by reviews.

- *Evaluation* – This is an opportunity to learn from practice by establishing what we did well (so that we can build on our strengths) and what we could have done better (to facilitate learning from experience). This again involves revisiting the assessment, as this will form the basis of our evaluation. (Chapter 6 looks at evaluation in much more detail.)

Each of these stages in the process is discussed in more detail in Chapters 19, 20 and 22 of *People Skills*. You are not expected to read each of Chapters 20 and 22 now, but you should find it helpful to look at them when you have more time, as they should cast a lot of light on the different aspects of the social work process.

Systematic practice

The notion of 'systematic practice' is one that we have already encountered. It is based on the principle that it pays dividends to keep a clear focus on what we are doing and why, asking the three key questions:

- What are you trying to achieve?
- How are you going to achieve it?
- How will you know when you have achieved it?

This is presented as a helpful framework to guide practice in general, but it can be seen to be particularly helpful in relation to assessment. We can see how each of the three questions relates to assessment in the following ways:

- *What are you trying to achieve?*
  Clearly this is an important question to consider as part of the assessment. It involves considering what needs remain unmet, what problems remain to be solved and so on. This question therefore acts as a focus for the assessment and helps to avoid the pitfall of simply gathering a lot of information, with no clarity about what needs to be done (see the section on 'Pitfalls' below).

- *How are you going to achieve it?*
  This question relates to the development of a strategy for achieving the identified objectives. Or, to put it another way, if the first question establishes the destination we want to arrive at, this second question is geared towards clarifying what route we intend to take – how we intend to try and get there.

- *How will you know when you have achieved it?*
  It is possible to be very vague in answering the first two questions, but this third one helps to pin things down more specifically by clarifying what success is expected to look like – that is, how we will recognise whether or not we have succeeded. For example, in response to the first question, we could answer: 'To support this person through a difficult time'; and to the second: 'By visiting on a regular basis'. Such vague responses are not really helpful as they do not give us a clear enough picture. The third question, though, will reveal this vagueness, as we need to be far more specific if we are going to be able to answer the third question.

Exercise 4.2

Choose a piece of work that you are currently involved with and consider it in terms of the three key questions of systematic practice. Ask yourself: what you are trying to achieve; how you intend to achieve it; and how you will know when you have achieved it. Think this through carefully.

The skills involved

There is no doubt that assessment is a very skilful process, and it is worth identifying what sort of skills are involved so that we can appreciate what goes into the process. The following skills are some of the main ones we draw upon in undertaking an assessment. However, the list is certainly not a comprehensive or exhaustive one.

Information gathering

Our senses are constantly bombarded with far more information than we can comfortably cope with, and so we are necessarily selective in terms of what information we take on board. Consequently, when we are gathering information as part of an assessment, we have to draw on our skill in judging what information is relevant and what is not. This involves keeping a clear focus and not gathering information for the sake of it 'just in case it proves useful later'. This is not only wasteful of time and effort, it can also distort the picture *and* amount to an intrusion into someone's privacy and therefore an infringement of civil liberties. The basis of our information gathering therefore needs to be 'need to know' rather than 'nice to know'.

Communication

In order to gather information and then make use of that information as part of a process of helping, we need to be able to communicate clearly and effectively. Our communication skills are therefore called upon as part of the process of assessment. This applies at a written level, too, as assessments need to be written down for the benefit of others involved in the process and for those who may be involved in the future and who will rely on historical records (today's assessment will be tomorrow's historical record). Recording skills are part of the repertoire needed for high-quality assessment, as poor recording will have the effect of undermining good work done.

Analysis

Because of the potential amount of information available and the dangers of 'not seeing the wood for the trees', analytical skills are an important part of assessment. Analysis involves identifying the key elements of a situation and recognising significant patterns and interrelationships. It is part of the process of making sense of a set of circumstances by establishing the basic components and the links between them. Analytical skills do not come easily to some people, and so it is necessary to persevere and develop them over a period of time. Some people are able to recognise patterns straight away, while others may look very carefully at a situation and not find anything that strikes them as a significant issue or pattern.

If you find that you struggle to develop analytical skills, it is recommended that you enlist the support of a colleague who is good at analysis and ask him or her to look at a situation with you so that you can see how he or she goes about it. You may wish to do this with more than one person, as different people tend to have different 'styles' of analysis and there may be something you can learn from each of them.

Planning

As we have seen, assessment involves developing a picture of the current situation and then deciding together how best to move forward. Chapter 5 is devoted to the process and skills of planning and so we will not comment on it further here, except to note that the discussion above of systematic practice applies also to planning.

Partnership

As we saw in Chapter 3, partnership is a central principle and value of social care. The skills involved in partnership are very relevant indeed to assessment. This is for two reasons:

1. Assessment is the beginning of the helping process, and so a failure to 'engage' with people at this stage does not bode well for working in partnership throughout the remainder of the work you will be undertaking together.
2. The remaining stages of the process hinge on the assessment undertaken, and so failure to take account of the service user's perspective at this point is likely to mean that the remaining stages are off target in terms of what you are, or should be, trying to achieve.

Partnership skills are therefore a fundamental part of effective assessment work.

Promoting equality

The significance of discrimination and oppression as factors to be aware of and as problems to be tackled was identified in Chapter 2. They are also, of course, very relevant to assessment, as they can easily come to feature at this stage and therefore have a detrimental effect on the overall process of helping. This can be seen to apply in three main ways, as follows:

1. *Social location* – People's 'social location' (that is, where they are located in society in terms of their class, gender, ethnic group and so on) is likely to be a significant feature of their situation in terms of:
   – their identity and sense of what groups they belong to;
   – their experience of life and their attitudes towards it, particularly in relation to their experience of oppression;
   – their perceptions of the worker;
   – their perception of what the problems are and what they see as potential solutions; and so on.

2. *Sources of problems* – Many problems will arise as a result of discrimination directed at members of certain groups. There are clear links between many of the problems that social care workers encounter and patterns of discrimination and oppression in the wider society (sexism, racism, a patronising attitude towards disabled people, a dismissive attitude towards older people and so on – Neil Thompson, 2006b).
3. *Sources of support* – There are many potential sources of support that people can draw upon, depending on which forms of discrimination they are subject to. For example, there are women's groups, black groups, disability pressure groups and so on that could be drawn upon to provide help and support for people to assist them in countering oppression. We therefore need to avoid becoming 'precious' and assuming that the problem is one that we need to solve – putting someone in touch with an appropriate supportive network may well be far more constructive and effective.

It is important to recognise the significance of discrimination and oppression at the assessment stage, as mistakes made here – false or discriminatory assumptions, for example – may have a very detrimental effect indeed on the work that is subsequently undertaken. It is therefore essential that assessment takes on board the important value of promoting equality.

Balancing positives and negatives

Social care workers can realistically be described as 'professional problem solvers'. One occupational hazard associated with this is the tendency apparent at times to concentrate on the negative side of things – to be tuned in to problems, weaknesses and threats without giving adequate attention perhaps to the positives. It is therefore important to guard against this unduly negative tendency by ensuring that we take account of not only weaknesses and threats but also strengths and opportunities.

This can be achieved by undertaking what is known as a SWOT analysis (see Thompson, 2006b for an account of how this can be used). This involves systematically identifying (in partnership with the service user) the **S**trengths, **W**eaknesses, **O**pportunities and **T**hreats – that is, looking at each of these areas in turn in order to ensure that we get a more balanced picture that takes account of the overall situation, rather than one that is predominantly negative.

This balanced approach that incorporates the strengths and opportunities inherent in a particular situation is not only important for the sake of accuracy and completeness, it also helps to instil a positive, constructive approach geared towards empowerment, rather than a negative, defeatist approach that can encourage 'learned helplessness' and an unduly negative and pessimistic attitude.

Exercise 4.3

Identify a situation you are involved with at the moment. (It may be a work situation or something in your private life – just any situation where you are trying to resolve some problem or deal with some issue.) Take a sheet of paper and draw a line down the middle and another across the middle, so that the paper is divided into four sections. Label the sections as follows:

- Top left: Strengths
- Top right: Weaknesses
- Bottom left: Opportunities
- Bottom right: Threats

You now have the basis of a SWOT analysis. Think carefully about the situation and identify the various strengths, weaknesses, opportunities and threats, recording them on the appropriate section of the page. Having this opportunity to practise a 'dry run' of a SWOT analysis should help to prepare you for using it in practice as part of the process of assessment.

Assessment pitfalls

Gathering too much information

As noted earlier, the basis of information needs to be 'need to know', not 'nice to know'. However, a common assessment pitfall is for workers to be led by anxiety into gathering far more information than they need. Worrying that 'I might miss something crucial' can lead people into going overboard on the amount of information they want to have available before they feel comfortable with the situation and ready to make sense of it and move towards action planning.

Drawing a line between what is relevant, useful information and what is superfluous or intrusive can at times be difficult, and there are few if any hard and fast rules about what should be in which category. However, what can be helpful in identifying this boundary line is to keep a clear focus on the *purpose* of the information gathering. For example, if you are a worker in a residential or day services setting and you are trying to get to know someone as part of an initial assessment in order to work out how best you can relate to this person, you will want to gather the sort of information that will give you a picture of their personality, their background, their likes and dislikes and so on. However, if you are undertaking a particular assessment relating to a specific issue (a particular problem or worrying situation, for example), your information gathering is likely to be much more focused, concentrating on the factors that you see as particularly relevant to the situation concerned.

It is also important not to forget that you are working in partnership, and that the service user will also give you some very significant clues as to what they believe to be relevant – and, of course, they know far more about the situation and their response to it than you do. It is therefore important to have our listening skills finely tuned and fully functional when undertaking an assessment so that we do not miss important messages service users are trying to give us.

Service-led assessment

The NHS and Community Care Act 1990 was intended to move away from the problem of service-led assessments by emphasising the importance of needs-led assessment. What this means is that we should not base our assessment on what services are available, but rather on what is needed. If our assessment is geared only towards the availability of existing services, then we will find it difficult to:

- Identify unmet need and the limitations of existing provision;
- Consider more creative ways of meeting needs and solving problems;
- Develop new services.

Needs-led services, by contrast, help us to understand:

- How existing provision may be helpful;
- How new approaches outside of conventional service provision may need to be drawn upon;
- What new services or other problem-solving approaches may need to be developed in the medium to long term.

We therefore have to be careful to ensure that we are not allowing our assessment practices to become exercises in trying to treat service users as if they were pegs that we are trying to fit into predetermined holes. This is not only likely to be ineffective, but is also an oppressive and dehumanising way of working.

Relying on stereotypes

The point has already been made that our senses are exposed to an immense amount of information on a daily basis and that we have to select which bits of information we see as relevant or important. One way in which the human mind undertakes this process of selection is through the use of broad categories or 'typifications' – we regard particular things as 'typical' of a broader category, and this helps us to process the information more efficiently. For example, when we see a car, we do not necessarily concentrate on the unique characteristics of that particular car. We are much more likely simply to see it as one example of the broader category or typification of 'car'. Typifications are therefore helpful ways of processing a large amount of information.

However, we have to make sure that we do not allow typifications to become stereotypes. A stereotype is a fixed and rigid form of typification, one that we tend not to change despite evidence to challenge our assumptions. For example, if we operate on the basis of the sexist stereotype that women talk more than men, we are likely to fail to recognise that, in reality, this is not the case – who talks more, men or women, depends very much on the circumstances, and so the sweeping generalisation that women are more talkative than men is a stereotype (a typification that we hold onto, despite evidence to show that this is not appropriate).

It is clearly important, then, to recognise that a reliance on stereotypes when undertaking an assessment is highly problematic, and indeed a very dangerous form of practice.

Magical thinking

By 'magical thinking' what we mean is the tendency to assume that by identifying a problem or an unmet need, that somehow, as if by magic, this will lead to the problem being resolved or the need being met. To be fair, it is important to recognise that, sometimes, simply becoming aware of a problem is enough to lead to its resolution – for example, when someone becomes aware of a particular aspect of their behaviour that is causing problems, the very fact of becoming aware of this can lead to sufficient self-awareness to curb that particular form of behaviour. However, this applies to a particular type of situation and is not applicable to the vast majority of situations where identifying the problem is only the first step towards tackling it.

An assessment should therefore be seen as not just an exercise in understanding the situation that needs to be addressed – it also involves establishing what needs to be done. Problem formulation needs to be followed by action planning. And, of course, the action plan needs to take account of the other elements of the assessment, the strengths and opportunities as well as the weaknesses and threats.

4.3 Assessing risk

What is risk?

Risk is a concept we all have to grapple with as part and parcel of our everyday lives. Whether we realise it or not, we are constantly making decisions about how, when and, indeed, whether to undertake a particular course of action in view of the relative risks involved. That is to say, we are constantly assessing our situation and making judgements based on what we expect, or hope, will follow from the course of action we eventually choose to take. Consequences are not necessarily positive, nor are they fixed or inevitable. We can not always predict what will happen if we choose, or choose not to, act in a particular way. When we talk about risk, we are considering the possibility of something dangerous or damaging ensuing from a course of action, or failure to take action in a given situation. In that case, then, there is probably very little in the modern world that could be considered risk free. Even wrapping oneself in cotton wool carries its own dangers – suffocation perhaps!

Of course, if we stopped to analyse the possible negative consequences of every action we proposed to take, we would probably get no further than the bedroom door each day before having to return to bed – a phenomenon sometimes known as 'paralysis by analysis'. In order to go about our business we often take for granted the risks that are involved, assuming that everything will be fine because it always has been before. It is often only when an accident occurs that we realise the risks we have been taking. As a result, we sometimes take action to reduce the risk of those harmful consequences occurring again. For example, following a serious car accident, some people may choose never to drive again. Others may recognise the risks involved but continue to take them, because the choice to give up driving might involve other risks – for example, losing one's means of getting to work – in order to earn one's livelihood. For most people the answer is not to attempt to reduce the risk of adverse consequences happening to nought per cent by refusing to take part in everyday living, but to find a balance between taking risks and enjoying the lifestyle of our choosing, complete with the risks that lifestyle involves. Some people are happier to take risks than others – indeed, some people get a 'buzz' from risk taking and claim it enhances their enjoyment of life.

Exercise 4.4

You might like to take a few minutes here to consider what risks you take in order to get yourself to work, and those you encounter once you get there. Are any of them avoidable? What might be the consequences of your choosing not to take those risks?

Precisely because risk taking is largely a matter of personal choice, it is important to consider the role of values in this context. For example, who decides what is risky and what is not? Indeed, can we quantify risk at all? We will look at this further in the following section, but it is worth reminding ourselves here that risk is not a fixed entity. It cannot be classified and quantified into a list of 'things that constitute risk', which people can refer to when assessing a situation. It varies from situation to situation and over time.

Let us consider the debate about the harmful effects of being overweight, for example. Obesity is not considered to be a health risk in some cultures. In fact, it is considered to be a desirable and attractive feature. In others it is considered to be a dangerous choice of lifestyle and is discouraged. Similarly, attitudes about what constitutes risk are not consistent over time. For example, in the nineteenth century, it was not considered damaging to young children's physical and emotional health for them to work long hours in mills and factories, whereas the risk of damage from unprotected machinery and lack of time set aside for play activity and emotional development is not accepted in today's climate.

If, then, daily life involves an ongoing process of balancing possible advantages against possible disadvantages in order to produce a favourable outcome, how can we help those people who either lack the insight to recognise the risks they might be taking or are particularly vulnerable to accidents or abuse – that is, those who are deemed to be 'at risk'? In the field of social care we are often working with vulnerable people, to whom we owe a duty of care by virtue of their definition as service users or residents. Protection from risk is a major feature of social care work, and one that carries an onus of responsibility and accountability. It is important that we are able to account for decisions we may make on other people's behalf, and therefore need to approach risk assessment in the same way we would approach any other form of assessment: systematically. We will look more at the mechanics of risk assessment in a later section, but before doing so we would wish to flag up the following points.

Can we measure risk?

The short answer to this question has to be no, in that there are too many variables involved for anyone to be able to classify what constitutes a particular level of risk in any given situation. As Parton *et al.* (1997) comment:

> *Risk does not arise from a single causal factor but a combination of multiple interacting elements located at the individual, family, community and societal levels. Not only does the significance of factors vary over time and space, but there are a variety of pathways to abuse.*

(p. 55)

It would be reassuring if it were possible to quantify and classify risk in a precise and scientific way, so that we could anticipate events, and hopefully prevent those to whom we owe a duty of care and protection from coming to harm. However, because we are dealing with people, rather than things, issues such as morality, emotion and self-determination 'complicate' the process of risk assessment and management, and a strictly scientific or 'positivistic' approach is therefore not helpful. Nor is it helpful to go to the other extreme and leave everything to chance, relying on guesswork to come up with the 'right' answer when undertaking risk assessments. Again we return to the balancing act, which More (1997) reminds us about. For example, he suggests that we sometimes compromise our own safety in the interests of providing what we feel to be a better service – taking a potentially violent service user out to a pub without a back-up team of colleagues 'just in case', or travelling unaccompanied to an isolated property in order to discuss sensitive issues with an emotionally volatile service user because he or she has requested to see you alone. Similarly, from a service user's point of view, lessening the chances of possible harm may be beneficial in one sense, but harmful in another. For example, it could be said that preventing an elderly resident of a care home from helping in the kitchens could reduce the likelihood of accidents in the form of burns, scalds or falling on sharp objects. This may be so, but protecting him or her in that way might be harmful in another sense, perhaps by increasing the risk of depression or low self-esteem, which might have been prevented by allowing that person to reciprocate in the care-giving relationship – perhaps by baking and sharing scones or cakes.

   If it is not possible to have 'absolute' guidelines on what constitutes risk, and each situation has to be weighed up individually, perhaps the most useful form of guidance would be to have a framework which could help us to organise our thoughts and stimulate us to seek out and analyse the information we need in order to make informed decisions about risk management. We will look at such a framework in the next section, but before we move on, we need to remind ourselves that we will never be able to eliminate risk entirely, nor should we be expected to. As we have already highlighted, it is often the case that reducing one risk factor throws another into prominence. The best we can hope for is to achieve a balance between reducing the risk of possible harm to a minimum without denying the person we are trying to protect the right to as 'normal' a life as possible. In order to be able to do this we need to be absolutely clear about what outcome we are trying to achieve, so that we can best plan how to get there – that is, to approach the assessment systematically, as discussed earlier in this chapter. In the next section we will look at a model of risk assessment which offers us just that sort of guidance, and discuss some of the issues around the actual risk assessment process. Before doing so it might be useful to undertake Exercise 4.5 in order to have the opportunity to think a little more around the need to see risk assessment as a process of finding an acceptable balance.

Exercise 4.5

Identify a situation (or imagine one) in which you have felt it necessary to prevent someone in your care from undertaking a particular activity or course of action. Consider the following questions:

1. What harm did you anticipate occurring, and what evidence did you use to make this judgement?
2. Was the service user involved in a discussion about the risk he or she was intending to take?
3. Can you think of any ways in which the service user might have 'lost out' by the decision not to proceed with the activity?
4. Was the decision a difficult one to make? If so, might a risk assessment model have helped to clarify your thoughts and provided evidence for your eventual decision?

Assessing risk

Before moving on to look at the early, but still very useful, model that Brearley (1982) proposes as an aid to risk management, we would want to highlight the following concepts as key issues:

- *Clarity* – The phrase 'at risk' is often used without the exact nature of the risk being spelt out. Vulnerable people are often referred to our care facilities, or support networks, having been designated as 'at risk in the community' or as 'posing a risk to the community', without any form of clarification. For example, what is the person at risk of? By whose definition? Is the risk constant or only in particular circumstances? Without clarification, the process of risk assessment is impossible to undertake fairly and effectively. Brearley's model will help us to think around the type of information we need to elicit in order to assess risk, but it is not the only literature on the subject. Littlechild and Blakeney (1996) remind us that we need to differentiate between what is *anticipated* risk (something that may happen – a perceived risk) and what is *actual risk* (something that has happened that may happen again). Being able to differentiate between the two is likely to make for a more appropriate outcome. The same authors also warn of the dangers of *exaggerating* risk. Whilst clarity is of paramount importance in ensuring that we do not do our service users a disservice when undertaking risk assessments, it is also a vital consideration when we consider our own vulnerability to our decisions being challenged.

- *Accountability* – When we are placed in the situation of owing someone a duty of care, we are also placed in the position of being accountable for the decisions we make in that role. As caregivers we are required to use our assessment skills to make decisions about the management of risk, and we do not always make the right one. Sometimes service users come to some form of harm, which, with hindsight could have been prevented. Let us consider the case of James, a ten-year old with brittle bones, who might not have fallen from the tree if the garden had been placed out of bounds to him. It had been considered unfair to have confined him indoors to a padded chair, as this would have severely impaired his enjoyment of life and his emotional and social development. Faced with the accusation that you, as officer-in-charge on the day of the accident, placed James 'at risk', by allowing him to play outdoors, you might find yourself having to account for that decision. The ability to be able to account for your actions, or lack of action, by showing how you had systematically assessed the risk situation prior to your decision is likely to stand you in good stead, whereas 'it seemed like a good idea at the time' would do very little for your professional credibility if there were to be legal repercussions or an official inquiry. Nobody can expect you to be totally infallible, and decisions are sometimes taken which lead to, or fail to prevent, harmful consequences. What is expected of you is that you make professional judgements based on your investigation into what is known about the situation and its participants. Clarity of thought and recording is therefore paramount in risk assessment.

- *Partnership* – As we discussed earlier, risk taking is an integral part of daily living, and something most of us do in the interests of having an interesting and fulfilling life. For some of our service users, the ability to make informed choices about risk is not an option. For example, people with advanced dementia are deemed to be unaware that they are placing themselves, or others, in situations of risk, and the legal system allows for others to make decisions on their behalf – guardianship, enduring power of attorney and so on. Babies and very young children may also have decisions made for them if the level of risk they are under is deemed to be unacceptable. In other circumstances, although the service user may be perceived as being very vulnerable, self-determination should not be overlooked in the interests of protection. Once again we return to the balancing act which is risk assessment. Whilst there may be a duty of care, good practice suggests that there is also a duty to empower, and the two may conflict. Including the service user, wherever possible, in the debate about risk-taking can provide the assessor with information about his or her needs and abilities and can also help the service user to appreciate the assessor's viewpoint and any constraints he or she might be under. Of course, as caregivers we are in the business of preventing our service users from coming to any harm. But if, in the process, we make their lives bland and unstimulating, are we not also doing them harm? Listening to them and involving them in decisions about risk management allows us a different perspective and upholds the principle of working together that we focused on in Chapter 3. It can also help us to practise in an anti-discriminatory way, heightening our awareness of cultural difference and challenging us to consider that we may be assessing risk according to our own value judgements, without considering that the service user might not be perceiving a situation according to those same values.

- *Cultural considerations* – It is important to remember that risk is not an absolute concept, but a social construction, being interpreted differently in different cultural contexts. Arguments have been put forward that cultural and religious perspectives on the acceptability of certain practices such as enforced clitoridectomy should be taken on board when assessing whether someone is 'at risk'. However, to refuse protection to a child in such circumstances, on the grounds that it is not considered abusive within his or her own culture, can be viewed as discriminatory, in that the child would not be offered the same degree of child protection intervention as any other child living in the UK. So, whilst risk has to remain a relative concept, it has to be recognised that the requirements of the law outweigh such cultural consider-ations. Parton *et al.* (1997) offer a more in-depth discussion on this subject and Parekh (2006) explores the contradiction between respecting the worldviews of others while upholding the right to not respect their choices if we find them 'perverse, outrageous or unacceptable' (p. 176).

- *Review* – As with any other form of assessment, it is important to remember that situations change. It is not enough to undertake an assessment of risk, intervene or otherwise on the basis of one's judgement, and then leave it at that. The very factor which may have precipitated a risk assessment may be resolved quite quickly and no longer be an issue a short time later. For example, an elderly person might be admitted to residential care on the grounds of being at risk of malnutrition and self-neglect – unable to feed, dress or cope with any of his or her personal care needs because of being in a highly confused state. If that person's confusion had been caused by the onset of a virulent chest or urine infection, the confusion might have been temporary and, within days, one might anticipate the person being back to his or her previously competent state. Review is therefore a fundamental part of the process and one which systematic practice upholds in the third question which asks of our intervention: 'how will we know when we have achieved it?'.

We will now go on to look at the model Brearley offers as an aid to organising our thoughts and information when assessing risk. It is one that can be applied across all service user groups and serves to remind us about some of the issues we have highlighted. The main points are as follows:

1. *Identify the cultural, racial and religious context of the situation.*
   It is important to begin with an understanding of the context in which we are working, as this is likely to have a crucial bearing on how we deal with the situation. A false assumption at this stage (about someone's religious beliefs, for example) could have major implications in so far as it could totally invalidate later aspects of the situation.
2. *List the dangers involved.*
   A danger is something we are trying to avoid, or fear might happen (perhaps a fall or a non-accidental injury). It is suggested that we prioritise these concerns at this point, identifying which ones we are particularly concerned about.
3. *List the hazards in the case.*
   In this context a hazard is defined as something which might lead to the danger you have identified becoming a reality (perhaps an ill-maintained staircase, or the presence of a violent adult in a household with young children).
4. *Identify the hazards as either:*
   (a) *predisposing* – something that creates vulnerability on an ongoing basis, such as dementia or a learning disability. It may not place the person in particular danger at a specific time but may be thrown into significance by a situational hazard.
   (b) *situational* – defined as something specific which happens and has an immediate effect on the danger identified earlier, perhaps a kitchen fire or a child accidentally damaging some property during play.
5. *Identify and list the strengths in this situation.*
   Strengths can be defined as factors which could serve to make the danger less likely to occur. Regular visits from a supportive family member might be an example of this.
6. *Identify what other information you believe to be necessary.*
   Based on the other information you have analysed this far, you should be able to work out what else you need to know in order to be able to do your risk assessment. For example, you may need to establish whether someone you think poses a threat to a vulnerable service user's safety is permanently resident with him or her, or visits only occasionally. You might also need the opinion of a colleague about, for example, a service user's intellectual capacity to make their own judgements. It might be as simple as finding out when that staircase is going to be fixed.
7. *Indicate the decisions you feel should be taken.*
   In addition to helping you through the assessment process and giving you confidence in your own judgement, the ability to be able to demonstrate that process to others in written form is likely to do wonders for your professional credibility.

Exercise 4.6

Identify a situation in which you have had to decide whether to take action in the face of a perceived risk. Go through the steps suggested in Brearley's model and consider how useful you found it.

Rights and risk

In Chapter 2 we discussed service users' right to self-determination. In situations where someone has the capacity to make their own judgements about risk then this should be respected. It would be unfair, and indeed discriminatory, to deny someone the right to take risks merely because he or she were, perhaps, old or disabled, on the grounds that the potential for risk was perceived to be greater than for his or her younger, non-disabled counterparts. We have a role to play in empowering our service users with the knowledge and skills they require in order to make decisions for themselves, rather than always being directed by others. However, we have talked too about the duty of care that we also owe to vulnerable service users – the duty to protect them from harm or disadvantage. As Carson (1996) comments:

> Basically, we all owe duties of care to those whom we can, being reasonable about it, foresee we might damage by an act or an omission. Hence you owe a duty of care to your client. It goes with the relationship. Why is the other person a 'client' other than because a particular propensity to harm is foreseen?

(p. 5)

As you can see, there is the potential for conflict here if we also want to uphold the principle of empowerment. Giving people rights may place them in situations where their safety might be compromised. It is a conflict which cannot ultimately be resolved, and one of the many dilemmas in the field of social care for which there is no 'right answer'. The best we can hope to achieve is a balance between the two, looking at whether the sacrifices that need to be made to ensure safety are worth the proposed benefits. This judgement can only be arrived at following a careful and ordered assessment of each situation and its unique factors.

Risk assessment pitfalls

This final section on risk assessment will serve to pull together some of the points we have already discussed and hopefully flag up a few more discussion points. You may be able to add a few of your own:

- *Rushing into things in a state of panic* – In potentially dangerous situations there is often a tendency to feel that we have to act immediately. This is usually not the case and taking time out to get an overview of the situation and to clarify the facts is usually time well spent. Without taking time to think things through, even though it may only be a few minutes, we may misinterpret situations and act inappropriately or unnecessarily.

- *Throwing everything at the situation* – Again, there is a tendency sometimes to feel that we need to respond in a major way when faced with a service user at risk, including calling in the police rapid-response unit and the parachute regiment! Of course, some situations can be very serious, requiring a multi-organisational response, but it is often the case that a very simple form of intervention is enough to defuse or even eradicate the risk altogether.

- *Swapping one set of risks for another* – We have said this far that the aim of risk management is to reduce potentially harmful consequences to a minimum. We need to be careful that we do not develop 'tunnel vision' in this respect, working towards a pre-determined goal without being aware of other things that are going on. It may be that 'solving' one issue may throw another risk situation into sharper focus. For example, persuading an elderly victim of physical abuse to enter residential care might resolve the risk of further physical injury, but might increase the risk of emotional and psychological harm that could occur as a result of having to give up his or her home and independence.

- *Taking all the responsibility on your own shoulders* – Risk management can be a very tricky business, and even with guidelines to follow, there are sometimes dilemmas which are difficult, if not impossible, to resolve. Using colleagues as 'sounding boards' can often open our eyes to different perspectives on a situation, or give moral support to our own judgement. Your employer should offer guidance and support if the management of risk is part of your job. If you do not have guidelines, or feel unprepared, then it is a matter to raise with your line manager.

- *Failure to review* – We might feel confident that, having carried out a risk assessment thoroughly and systematically, we have responded in an appropriate way and the risk element managed effectively. However, it is important that we do not forget that situations are fluid – things change and our intervention needs to be reviewed. For example, it might be necessary to provide 24-hour supervision for a mother in an acute psychotic state to prevent her newly born child from the risk of being harmed. But the level of risk is likely to fluctuate, and it would be totally inappropriate to intervene in such a way if the condition were resolved and the mother able to recognise and care adequately for her child.

- *Relying on someone else's definition of risk* – We have discussed already that we are accountable for our own actions and interventions, which means that we have to have confidence in our own judgements. These will have been arrived at with due regard to the values we see as important to uphold. Others may define risk in the context of a different set of values. That is not to say we should act independently of others, but nor should we take their interpretation at face value. Multidisciplinary collaboration on risk assessment can be extremely effective, and is considered to be an essential part of good practice in child abuse investigations. Whilst the perspectives and expertise of others can prove invaluable, they should be used as aids to, rather than substitutes for, our own assessments.

4.4 Conclusion

Assessment is clearly an essential and fundamental part of social care practice. It involves a number of skills and is beset by a number of pitfalls. It is not so much an exact science as an art or craft. It involves a number of people working together in a spirit of partnership to develop a picture of the current situation and drawing up plans for what needs to be done to tackle problems and build on strengths. It is the basis of the remaining stages of the social work process and therefore plays a crucial role in determining the success and appropriateness of much of what follows. Its importance should therefore not be underestimated, and the commitment of time, thought and energy needed to make it work should also be recognised as being of significant proportions.

Chapter 5

Planning Responses

5.1 Introduction

This chapter covers the important topic of planning in social care. The basic idea underpinning the chapter is that good practice is premised on effective planning – a clear and structured process of anticipating, and preparing for, future developments in the circumstances of service users and carers. It means that interventions need to relate to specific aims and objectives, so that positive benefits can be maximised and potential pitfalls can be avoided. The chapter explores issues relating to:

- *What is planning?* – understanding what is involved in the process of planning.
- *The life course* – appreciating the significance of human development and the different stages of life as they affect different people.
- *Meetings* – a major focus for planning processes and often not as helpful as they could be.
- *Pitfalls* – some of the many ways in which planning can be blocked, misguided or misused.

Social care involves identifying and responding to the needs and related problems of particular groups of people in society. Assessment begins this process and planning sustains it in so far as planning entails clarifying what needs to be done – planning how we are to respond to the situations we encounter.

5.2 What is planning?

The term 'planning' is one that is used in both a formal and informal sense. In a formal sense, it refers to meetings that are convened specifically to review current circumstances and identify what now needs to happen (review meetings, case conferences and so on). However, planning also goes on in an informal way outside of such formal meetings – day-to-day interactions with service users, for example. Deciding where to go, what to do; talking about hopes, fears and wishes; considering options; anticipating possible problems or conflicts; these are all part of the informal planning processes that go on in social care on a day-by-day basis. Planning, then, is both a formal process that occurs at set times according to recognised procedures and part and parcel of everyday practice. Indeed, it could be argued that an important ingredient of effective planning is the ability to make sure that what goes on at the informal level is fed into the formal process so that the latter is based, as far as possible, on a good understanding of the realities of the service user's life and current circumstances. This is, of course, an important foundation for working in partnership, a topic to which we shall return below.

Strategic thinking

An important basis for effective planning is the ability to think strategically. 'Strategy' is a term that is commonly used in management theory and practice, but it is also one which can be seen as very relevant to the caring professions (Egan, 2004). It refers to the route we choose in order to work towards our identified objectives or desired outcomes – our plan of action, as it were.

In this sense, strategic thinking is very similar to, and closely associated with, the logic underpinning systematic practice, particularly in relation to the second of the three key questions (as discussed in earlier chapters and in *People Skills*): How are you going to achieve it? (that is: how are you intending to fulfil your objectives?). This can be illustrated as follows:

1. What are you trying to achieve?

   =

   What is your desired outcome/your intended destination?
2. How are you going to achieve it?

   =

   What strategies are available/what routes can you use?
3. How will you know when you have achieved it?

   =

   How will you evaluate the effectiveness of the chosen strategy?

Strategic thinking, then, is the type of thought that has to go into considering the various strategies that are available to us in trying to achieve our desired outcomes. It involves:

- *a degree of imagination* – being able to develop a vision of the possible ways forward;
- *'helicopter vision'* – the ability to develop an overview of a situation, to get the 'big picture', rather than simply focus on a narrow range of issues;
- *communication skills* – the capacity to convey your views of the situation to others while being able to take their views on board, thus contributing to partnership.

The emphasis on systematic practice in earlier chapters (in relation to assessment, for example) should act as a useful foundation on which to build the type of strategic thinking on which effective planning is premised. This is an example of the type of analytical skill that is closely associated with expectations of *professional* practice associated with Level 4 and higher level professional qualifications in social work.

Exercise 5.1

Think of a situation at work that you have dealt with in work where your plans came to fruition, that is, where you achieved what you set out to. Think carefully about the situation and see if you can come up with other possible ways in which you could have achieved the same results. In other words, what other strategies would have been available to you?

Anticipating the future

We cannot know exactly what will happen but we can, of course, try to identify trends and anticipate certain events or patterns. It may initially sound quite daunting to learn that, as part of our work in social care, we are expected to anticipate the future. However, when we think more carefully about this, we should quickly realise that this is a skill that we already possess and an activity that we carry out regularly in our everyday lives. Consider, for example, the following tasks and activities that occur on a not infrequent basis:

- meeting someone at the station;
- preparing for a meeting;
- arranging a social event such as a party;
- deciding what clothes to wear for a particular trip or outing;
- undertaking a journey.

Of course, when you look closely at the items on this list, you should be able to recognise that, in one way or another, they all involve anticipating the future – trying to predict what might happen so that we are ready to deal with it. This may involve drawing on 'planning tools', such as bus or train timetables, meeting agendas, maps and so on. But, however we tackle these activities, they none the less involve a degree of anticipation on our part. The important point to recognise, therefore, is that we are already skilled and experienced at anticipating the future. Our learning task, then, is not to start from scratch, but rather to build on our existing skills – to enhance and consolidate them so that we can become even more skilful at anticipating what is likely to happen.

Shaping the future

Forewarned is forearmed is a well-known saying – and, of course, one that makes a lot of sense. If we are aware that something is likely to happen, we can prepare for it, or even try to prevent it from happening. Anticipating the future is therefore an important part of good practice. A less well-known saying but a none the less important one deriving from management education and training is that: 'A competent manager *anticipates* the future, but an excellent manager *shapes* the future'. We can adapt this saying from its management context to a social care one, as we would argue that high standards of practice in working with people in a social care context also involves shaping the future – having a constructive influence on what happens and working towards positive outcomes.

In effect, this is the essence of planning – being able to use our understanding, skills and experience to anticipate the future as realistically as we can in order to help shape what happens. This can be an extremely important factor in helping to empower service users (that is, to give them greater control over their lives). This is because the positive actions and attitudes of the worker towards the future can be a significant source of motivation, reassurance and support for the service user who, as a result of past negative experiences, may feel less than positive about what the future holds or what can be achieved. Our ability to work positively towards shaping the future can therefore be significant in generating confidence and a commitment to change. The lesson we can learn from this, then, is: our task is not only to anticipate the future but also to shape it – to play an active part in bringing about positive outcomes.

Exercise 5.2

Chapter 20 of *People Skills* addresses planning. Read that chapter now and then complete the exercise at the end of that chapter.

Promoting partnership

Shaping the future is not solely the worker's responsibility. It needs to be a shared endeavour – to be done in *partnership*. Planning is something that all concerned need to do *together*. This is because, as noted previously, people need to be involved if they are to take ownership and seek to make things work. Without this sense of ownership, there is a danger of creating dependency by leaving the responsibility for the problem-solving process with the worker – hence creating a barrier to progress for the service user and a potential source of stress for the worker. Also, as Egan (2004) comments, working to goals that have not been jointly agreed on and therefore 'owned' by a service user introduces the potential for someone who fails to make progress to blame others for that lack of progress. Partnership should therefore be seen as a fundamental basis for planning.

One way of making sure that partnership is promoted is to avoid making decisions *for* people, even where options are very limited or where other constraints are operating. Adams (1994) captures this point well when he comments that:

> Decisions should not be made in advance and then forced on people. Even where the options are limited, efforts should be made to negotiate with them and offer them real choices based on their own experiences and wishes.

(p. 37)

Of course, this is not the only way in which partnership can be promoted in planning responses to identified needs and problems. Exercise 5.3 is designed to help you explore the range of other steps that can be taken in order to reinforce a spirit of partnership. Take some time now to tackle Exercise 5.3 (jointly with one or more colleagues, if you wish) before proceeding with the rest of the text.

Exercise 5.3

What other opportunities are available for making planning a process based on partnership? What are the practical steps that can be taken to encourage effective collaboration?

5.3 The life course

The term 'life course' is one that is used as a shorthand to describe the psychology of human development, the range of factors that affect, shape and influence our development as we grow and change throughout our lives. This is an important area of study as far as planning is concerned, in so far as how we respond to a particular individual will depend, to a certain extent at least, on the point which he or she has reached in the life course – that is, the stage of development. It is therefore important that, in planning responses, we take account of life course issues. An understanding of the life course can provide a helpful backcloth for appreciating the context of people's behaviour, attitudes and responses. This understanding will not provide us with all that we need to know, but it is certainly a useful starting point.

Ages and stages

The most common approach to the life course is what is known as the 'ages and stages' approach. This refers to the range of theoretical perspectives that have in common an emphasis on dividing the life course up into different sections or stages, each with their own characteristics. Probably the best known ages and stages theory is that of Erik Erikson who argued that the life course was best understood in terms of eight stages (Erikson, 1977). These can be summarised as shown in the chart below.

The basic idea underpinning this and related models is that, as we pass through the life course, we move from one stage to another, facing new challenges and new opportunities as we pass from one to the next. Such a way of looking at human development has advantages and disadvantages, including the following:

Advantages:	It provides an overview of general patterns shared by large numbers of people, allowing comparisons to be drawn.
	It helps us to distinguish between the different needs people have at different stages during their life course.
Disadvantages:	It can place too much emphasis on what is deemed 'normal' and can lead to differences being seen as problems.
	It pays insufficient attention to broader social factors, such as class, race and gender.

1. **Basic trust**
   vs.
   Basic mistrust

   The young baby needs to learn to trust first parents and then others.

2. **Autonomy**
   vs.
   Shame and doubt

   The young child needs to learn to think and act for him/herself, to develop self-control.

3. **Initiative**
   vs.
   Guilt

   The growing child needs to move towards independence and use initiative, albeit in a limited way.

4. **Industry**
   vs.
   Inferiority

   The young school child needs to learn the value and pleasure of achieving tasks.

5. **Identity**
   vs.
   Role confusion

   In the early stages of adolescence, a coherent sense of identity needs to be formed in preparation for adulthood.

6. **Intimacy**
   vs.
   Isolation

   The young adult needs to establish adult relationships and form a new generation of family life.

7. **Generativity**
   vs.
   Stagnation

   Maturity needs to be characterised by a sense of achievement, productivity and fulfilment.

8. **Ego integrity**
   vs.
   Despair

   In the later stages of life, we need to face up to the reality of death with dignity.

It is, of course, quite obvious that we should respond differently to, say a two-year old than we would to a twenty-two-year old, or a seventy-two-year old. However, there are (at least) three important points we should recognise here:

1. Although the major differences of age and development are quite obvious, there are also many differences that are much more subtle but which can be just as significant. For example, in adolescence, there can be major developmental changes (of an emotional nature, perhaps) within a matter of months. See also the discussion below of crisis and loss where the significance of certain developmental 'turning points' within the life course is pointed out.

2. We have to be wary of ageism in the sense of having stereotypical expectations of people because of their age. This is perhaps most easily recognised in relation to older people but can apply to any age group (Sue Thompson, 2005). The life course stages are only one part of understanding an individual and his or her 'biography'. We should be wary of seeing age-related expectations as rigid 'rules' or patterns that have to be followed. They may well be the starting point of our understanding but they should not

be the whole story. Indeed, to fail to recognise this could lead to very oppressive forms of practice in which people feel they are being forced into age-related strait-jackets rather than being dealt with as unique individuals.

3. Although people who are at the same stage in their life course will tend to have a lot in common, we should not allow this to distract our attention from the fact that they are also likely to have many differences. These will include social differences, such as class, race/ethnicity and gender, as well as more individualised differences such as personal preferences, values, lifestyle and so on. Again, it is important to recognise that we are dealing with individuals in the context of the life course and not simply with that context, as if individuals were just examples of that context.

Exercise 5.4

How would you see yourself in terms of the life course? How, at this stage in your development, are you different from how you used to be? How do you think you might change in the future? After considering these issues, what implications does this raise for how you might respond differently in future to the service users you work with?

Crisis, loss and growth

Implicit in the notion of the life course is the concept of 'transition', the movement from one stage or phase to the next. This is closely linked with the theme of crisis and loss. In order to understand growth and development we therefore need to have at least a basic understanding of crisis and loss.

A crisis can be defined as:

> . . . *a turning point, a situation which pushes our usual coping mechanisms beyond their usual limits of effectiveness and thus necessitates a different response, a different strategy for coping.*
>
> (Thompson, 1991: p. 4)

The term 'crisis', then, refers to a 'make or break' situation, one in which things cannot continue as they are – they will either get better or get worse. However, what also needs to be understood in looking at the concept of crisis is that a crisis is not necessarily the same as an emergency – although the two are often confused in practice. An emergency is a situation that has to be dealt with urgently, whereas a crisis may not. For example, someone may need urgent assistance in order to prevent a crisis arising but actually takes the situation in their stride. The emergency in this case, then, can be seen to *prevent* a crisis, rather than actually *be* a crisis. Similarly, many crisis situations are not emergencies. For example, an elderly person being admitted to a residential home on a permanent basis is likely to experience a crisis (a turning point in their life), even though the actual admission may have been planned many weeks in advance, therefore not constituting an emergency.

We have to be careful, then, not to confuse crises with emergencies. Sometimes, the two categories overlap, but often they are separate and quite distinct.

It is generally recognised that there are two types of crisis. One type is *situational* and is difficult to predict. This refers to events that are unexpected and not necessarily inevitable – they owe a lot to chance. Bereavements, accidents and so on would come into this category. The other type of crisis is a *developmental* one. This refers to crises that are linked to the life course, such as adolescence or the menopause. Such crises are far more predictable and often have a degree of inevitability.

From a planning point of view, this latter category is perhaps the more important because we have a much greater chance of predicting them and therefore being prepared for them. But even with situational crises, we can still undertake a degree of planning – for example, by getting to know how the person concerned is likely to respond to a particular crisis point if it were to arise. We may not be able to predict a bereavement, but we could get to know enough about the person to be able to support them through such a loss if it were to occur.

Closely linked to the idea of crisis is that of loss. Indeed, it could be argued that all crises involve a degree of loss as they involve, by definition, a change in the person's life and circumstances. Loss is an event that is generally linked to bereavement (that is, the loss of a person through death) and which produces a response in the form of grief and mourning. However, we should recognise that loss is a much broader concept. It can occur in a variety of ways, each of which can evoke grief and mourning. These include loss of:

- home;
- relationship (divorce/separation/admission to care);
- functional ability (through illness or disablement);
- trust (for example, through abuse);
- dreams and expectations;
- confidence or self-esteem;
- status;
- control; and
- hope.

Clearly, then, loss features in people's lives much more than we might have expected if we had limited our understanding of loss issues to the question of death and dying. The important conclusion we can draw from this is that, as far as planning is concerned, loss is likely to be a major feature for many people. It is therefore important that we understand at least the basics of how people respond to loss.

Although there are many theories of loss, one theme they have in common is that loss can produce a significant psychological reaction (grief) and also has to be seen in its social context (mourning). But note that we describe grief as a *psychological* response rather than simply an emotional response. This is because grief affects not only our emotions but also our thoughts (or cognitions) and our behaviour. 'Mourning' refers to the social dimension of loss and can be seen in terms of rituals or expected patterns of behaviour and response at a time of bereavement. Such rituals can be a major source of support and comfort when someone's life has been disrupted by a serious loss.

The subject of loss, grief and mourning is a major one and it is certainly beyond the scope of this chapter to cover it in sufficient detail. You would therefore do well to consult one or more of the major textbooks on loss, perhaps using the 'Guide to Further Learning' at the end of the book as a guide.

Exercise 5.5

How would you know that someone was grieving? How would you recognise the effects of loss on someone? How should you respond to someone who is grieving? What support would you need? Consider carefully your response to these questions.

5.4 Planning meetings

It was pointed out earlier that formal planning tends to occur by means of a meeting or series of meetings, in principle bringing together the relevant people to explore and agree what steps need to be taken. Although much attention is generally given to developing good practice in our interactions with service users, relatively little is given to the subject of meetings and how they should be conducted. This section of the chapter therefore looks at what is involved in developing good practice in the context of planning meetings.

Purpose and focus

Meetings, by their very nature, involve bringing together a number of people, often with different expectations or different wishes. The potential for conflict is therefore quite considerable. However, conflict does not have to be overt and clearly visible. It can often occur much more subtly, 'under the table', as it were. This is often referred to as a hidden agenda, a situation in which a power battle or struggle to 'win the day' goes on implicitly. It takes very little awareness to realise that this is a potentially very damaging situation from which a lot of harm can ensue, not least in terms of the lack of effectiveness that can be engendered by such power games.

The first conclusion we can draw about planning meetings therefore, is that we should be very wary of the danger of power battles 'hijacking' the meeting. One important way of doing this is to ensure that there is a very clear and strong focus on the purpose of the meeting – that is, on *planning*. Indeed, the need to keep a clear focus on the purpose of the meeting is a major part of good practice in so far as it can and should:

- avoid 'drift' and a sense of purposelessness which, as we have noted in earlier chapters, can easily become a feature of social care practice;

- help to keep the channels of communication open so that the necessary discussion and exchange of information is not inhibited;
- motivate the participants to keep concentrating and devoting their energies to the task in hand;
- make sure the limited time available is used to the best effect;
- prevent service users and less experienced participants from being discouraged from making a contribution.

Power battles are not the only obstacle to keeping a clear focus. Drift away from the purpose of the meeting can occur for a variety of reasons. For example, there may be too much emphasis on reviewing what has happened to date, thereby not leaving enough time to address what needs to happen in the future (it is, of course, far less risky to review the past and present than to plan for the future, so there may be an element of defensiveness involved where this problem arises). Also, there may be a conflict of interest between, say, a service user and a carer or there may be other difficult or painful issues that some people may prefer to avoid (deliberately or otherwise).

Of course, the person chairing the meeting ultimately has responsibility for ensuring that a clear focus on the purpose of the meeting is maintained. However, complete responsibility does not fall to this person alone. Each participant must share in the responsibility of ensuring a clear focus in order to maximise the chances of an effective meeting.

Using skills

Meetings involve various skills, and it could be argued that this applies to planning meetings even more so. Exercise 5.6 is geared towards helping you appreciate the skills involved in planning meetings. This should help to establish your own 'baseline'. That is, it should help you identify which of these important skills you have and which you feel you need to develop. The exercise is in two parts. The first addresses the skills involved in contributing to the effective use of meetings. The second focuses more specifically on the skills involved in planning meetings (for example, the skills involved in preparing and supporting any service users or carers who will be present).

Exercise 5.6

Part 1

Think about the various meetings you have attended. What skills were you able to draw on in order to play your part in these meetings? What skills have you witnessed other people using? Have you encountered meetings where there were problems because one or more people lacked a particular skill or skills? What were these?

Exercise 5.6

Part 2

Having considered the skills involved in meetings in general, focus now on the specific skills involved in planning meetings. What are these skills? Which of these do you already possess? Which do you need to develop?

Feel free to consult one or more colleagues in tackling this exercise.

5.5 Pitfalls of planning

Sadly, it is not uncommon for the planning process to go wrong. This can be for various reasons, including the following:

- The sheer complexity of a particular situation may make it very difficult indeed to undertake effective planning.

- A person's behaviour may be so volatile and unpredictable as to make planning very difficult, if not impossible.

- Workloads may make it difficult to find the time to give planning the attention it deserves.

- One or more people involved may not co-operate, thereby blocking the efforts of others.

The problems may arise as a result of one of these reasons or any combination of them. There are also many other obstacles that can get in the way, pitfalls that can lead to planning going astray. This section of the chapter therefore explores some of these pitfalls so that, wherever possible, these can be avoided.

I did it my way

This refers to the problem of pursuing one's own agenda and therefore not working in partnership. Planning is a multidisciplinary activity, and therefore brings with it considerable potential for conflict. One way of avoiding this conflict is to 'plough one's own furrow', to simply go one's own way and not involve others in planning. As discussed in Chapter 3, partnership is an approach to working that has to be carefully nurtured. If we do not take account of other people's perspectives in undertaking planning, we should not be surprised if partnership fails to materialise, leaving us to cope unassisted with a demanding task and possibly with a great deal of bad feeling on the part of those who have been excluded.

Although a particular individual (a key worker, perhaps) may have to take a lead role in planning, we should not confuse taking a lead role with simply doing it all yourself. Not only is the 'I did it my way' approach unhelpful for the service user and others involved, it also places extra pressure on the worker and leaves him or her with more to be blamed for if things go wrong.

Tramlines

Thinking in very narrow, restricted ways is also a problem when it comes to planning. As mentioned earlier, one of the skills of effective planning is the ability to 'get the big picture', to gain a broad overview of the situation and its possibilities. Also important is the ability to be imaginative and creative, to envisage a range of possible ways forward, rather than simply be limited by a narrow focus on a limited range of possibilities. A 'tramlines' approach with a restricted vision of future possibilities may well do a considerable disservice to a service user who is then faced with a narrower range of options than is strictly necessary.

This is not to say that 'anything goes'. There are, of course limits to what can be considered and what can be done. However, we should be wary of placing unnecessary restrictions by failing to be imaginative in creating a vision of the possible ways forward.

Vagueness and drift

A recurring theme in this series of chapters has been the need to keep a clear focus on what we are doing and why. This is an important theme to emphasise as it helps to prevent vagueness and drift. While this can be seen as an important principle of good practice in general, it is particularly relevant to planning, as vagueness and drift can undermine the whole process, leaving the people involved bedevilled with a lack of clarity.

One unfortunate consequence of vagueness and drift can be the tendency for people to become demotivated. If there is a lack of clarity and focus, situations can become unnecessarily confusing and complex, giving people more of a headache than they need to! Faced with this scenario of complexity and confusion, with a lack of clarity about how progress can be achieved, it is not surprising that some people at least may lose interest and commitment in taking things forward.

Unrealistic expectations

One very clear barrier to effective planning is the setting of unrealistic goals or targets. Goals that are attainable can be a very significant source of motivation, leading to a high level of commitment to improving the situation. However, goals that are out of reach will not only fail to motivate people but are also likely to *demotivate*, in the sense that they can leave the people concerned feeling that there is little point trying. Consequently, it is vital that, in agreeing what we should be aiming for, we should not be unrealistic in our expectations of what can be achieved.

Agreeing unrealistic goals can be damaging not only in the short term by demotivating people, but also in the longer term by undermining confidence and self-esteem. This can mean that longer-term goals may also not be achieved because the damage done in the short term has long-lasting consequences for the people so affected.

Projection

This is a concept associated with Freudian theory but also used much more widely. It refers to the process whereby an individual 'projects' their feelings onto another person. For example, someone who is anxious in a particular situation may assume that another person or persons in that situation are also anxious. We therefore have to be very wary, in the planning process, that we do not project our feelings onto the service user concerned. How we would react to a situation is not necessarily how he or she would react, and so there is a very real need to make sure that we are taking account of people's views and feelings, rather than simply assuming our response would also be their response.

Projection is an understandable trap to fall into, as we may have strong feelings about situations we encounter, but we must remember that these are *our* feelings, and are not necessarily shared by others involved.

Service-led planning

Resources are, of course, finite rather than unlimited. Consequently, we have to be aware of resource shortfalls in making plans. However, there is a danger in linking plans too closely to available resources. This is for three reasons:

1. This can distort the planning process. Instead of looking at what the person needs, we focus too much on what is or may be available. This can lead to a one-sided picture.
2. By not concentrating on needs, we will miss opportunities to identify gaps in service provision and therefore to inform policy makers of areas for development in future policy planning (individual case planning feeding into policy planning).
3. A narrow focus on available resources will deter imaginative or creative approaches to problem solving, encouraging the tramlines approach discussed above.

It should be clear, then, that the planning process should be needs led, rather than service led, in much the same way as assessment was presented in Chapter 4.

Ageism

As we have seen, planning involves taking account of the life course, so that we are able to understand the needs and circumstances of individuals in relation to their social and personal development. However, this is not to say that we should oversimplify the situation and attempt to understand individuals purely in relation to their age or development. This would amount to relying on ageist stereotypes. For example, issues of adolescent development would be very relevant to understanding a fifteen-year old's current circumstances and future plans. However, to see this fifteen-year old simply as an adolescent, with no account of his or her other characteristics, relationships or views would be to reduce a unique individual to the status of just one example of a broad category. This is clearly a very dehumanising thing to do, and therefore quite oppressive and not in keeping with the value base.

Hidden agenda

Ideally, the primary focus of planning should be the particular individual concerned and his or her needs, circumstances, strengths, rights and so on. However, it has to be acknowledged that social care operates in a complex organisational context, with several agendas having a bearing on processes and outcomes. A very real pitfall, therefore, is that of other agendas standing in the way of progress. For example, personality clashes, power battles, unresolved conflicts, unfinished business from previous encounters and so on can all have an effect – generally a very detrimental effect – on the planning process.

Keeping a clear focus on the planning agenda and not getting sidetracked by other agendas has to be recognised as both a very important task and a very difficult one. It requires a degree of awareness of complex organisational and political interactions and processes. It is not expected that social care staff should be experts on organisational dynamics and politics, but there is an expectation of at least a basic level of awareness (see Thompson, 2003b, Chapter 6).

5.6 Conclusion

Social care is a demanding type of work, physically, mentally and emotionally. It is also a type of work beset by all sorts of problems and pitfalls. And, on top of all this, staff are expected to anticipate or even shape the future! In effect, this is what planning amounts to.

However, it is to be hoped that this chapter has helped to provide some insights into how this can be done, as well as some confirmation of existing skills, knowledge and good practices. Clearly, it will not have given simple, straightforward answers, as no chapter can do that. As we noted in Chapter 1, the nature of social care is far too complex for this, as is the nature of learning and professional development. However, there has, we hope, been a further contribution to your development through studying this chapter, a further contribution to the development of reflective practice.

Chapter 6

Evaluation and Development

6.1 Introduction

We have now reached the final chapter, and so it is very appropriate that, as the final chapter, it is geared, in part at least, towards helping you to continue to learn throughout your career and not just while you are working towards a particular qualification.

The chapter concentrates on three sets of issues:

1. *Evaluating practice*: If we are to learn from our practice, we need to evaluate it – to stop and think about what worked well and what could have worked better. Evaluation is therefore an important process and worth the investment of time and effort it takes.
2. *Discrimination and oppression*: We emphasised in Chapter 2 the importance of recognising, and working to, the values that underpin professional practice in social care. Amongst these was anti-discriminatory practice; the steps needed to counter discrimination and oppression. Here we consider how we can ensure, as far as possible, that these values issues remain firmly on the agenda.
3. *Professional development*: The importance of continuing to learn and develop is receiving increasing recognition. This section of the chapter looks at why this is and explores how we can maximise the opportunities for continuing to learn and develop as we gain more experience and meet new challenges.

> Chapter 22 of *People Skills* is devoted to 'Review and Evaluation'. Read that chapter now before proceeding with this chapter.

6.2 Evaluating practice

Why evaluate?

There are various reasons why we should take the time and trouble to evaluate our work. These include:

- identifying our strengths so that we can gain job satisfaction from them and build on them;
- identifying weaknesses or areas for development so that we can be wary of potential pitfalls and, where possible, seek to turn weaknesses into strengths;
- recognising our accountability – taking some degree of responsibility for the outcome of our interventions;

- using opportunities to learn from experience. As we saw in Chapter 1, we do not automatically learn from experience – we have to reflect on that experience and relate it to our previous learning and understanding, and evaluation is a very helpful way of doing this.

A further important reason for evaluating our work is that of *professional credibility*.

A professional group that simply presses on with its day-to-day duties without ever stopping to evaluate how effectively it is operating is likely to lose credibility in the eyes of other groups who are more rigorous in the monitoring of standards and efforts to improve practice. And, of course, professional credibility is not simply a matter of status or prestige, it is – much more importantly – a question of influence and acceptance. We should not be surprised if others do not listen to us or take us seriously if we do not have the professional credibility to earn their respect. In undermining our own professional credibility, we thereby undermine our ability to do our jobs effectively and therefore do our service users a considerable disservice.

Types of evaluation

Shaw (1996) discusses three different types of evaluation. These are:

- *Evidence-based evaluation*: This type of evaluation relies on a number of measurement scales to gauge the effectiveness of particular interventions in terms of their outcomes. It is therefore a quantitative approach, with a strong emphasis on objectivity.

- *Empowerment evaluation*: This alternative approach rejects the idea that we can be objective and focuses instead on being both 'an onlooker in the stalls and a member of the cast, entering as a partner with the actors' (p. 8). It is concerned with understanding processes as well as outcomes, particularly processes that can lead to discrimination and oppression.

- *Reflective evaluation*: This relates to the notion of 'reflective practice', as discussed in Chapter 1. Evaluation can and should take place through a process of reflection both during practice ('thinking on your feet' or reflection-*in*-action) and afterwards (reflection-*on*-action). This involves a greater emphasis on participation on the part of service users. Reflection is not just a process of thinking but also involves taking on board other people's perceptions.

One common misunderstanding is that it is only the first form of evaluation that is valid because it is 'scientific'. As Shaw (1996) makes clear, this is an oversimplification of a very complex area, and so we should be very wary of dismissing empowering or reflective evaluation as unscientific. Each has a contribution to make. Exercise 6.1 should help you to appreciate this to some extent at least.

The main point to emphasise at this juncture is that there are different types of evaluation and evaluation is not simply a matter of applying strict scientific criteria in terms of defining problems and reviewing outcomes in such a way as to be able to measure them for the purpose of drawing statistical comparisons.

Evaluation is a complex subject, although we should note that practitioners do not need to be experts in the subject to be able to carry out evaluations and benefit from doing so.

Exercise 6.1

Consider the three types of evaluation described above. Can you identify ways in which you could (or already do) use each of the three forms of evaluation. Are there any aspects of your work where the outcomes can be measured? Are there opportunities for you to evaluate the processes that go on in practice (particularly in relation to discrimination and oppression)? Are you able to evaluate through reflection-*in*-action and reflection-*on*-action (to think on your feet as it is happening and stop and think afterwards)?

It may take you some time to work these out so do feel free to consult with colleagues and undertake this exercise together if you wish.

Giving and receiving feedback

An important part of keeping a clear view of our work and its impact is to receive feedback. Unless we are aware of how we are coming across to other people, we will not be able to gauge how well we are doing or how appropriate our actions and responses are. It is therefore important that we build in opportunities for receiving feedback. Exercise 6.2 is designed to help identify who should be involved and how the process can be facilitated.

While recognising the importance of receiving feedback, we should of course also acknowledge the important role of *giving* feedback. Social care is a team activity, and so it is necessary for us not only to take (in the sense of drawing on the benefits of other people's constructive feedback) but also to give (by offering helpful feedback to others). This can be seen to involve the following:

- Recognising a job well done and giving praise where it is due. We all benefit from having our efforts and our work appreciated. This can play an important part in creating a positive team atmosphere in which people are happy to support each other by recognising and openly acknowledging strengths. The more we do this for others, the more likely it becomes that they will do it for us.

- Pointing out mistakes to each other. Of course, this has to be done sensitively and tactfully! However, if we notice a colleague making a mistake, and we do not point this out to him or her, then we are doing that colleague a disservice. The trick here is being able to point out mistakes in such a way as to ensure that it does not come across as a criticism.

Clearly, what we are describing here is a fairly skilled set of activities, but ones which can be very valuable in promoting a supportive team atmosphere in which people are open and constructive, prepared to give helpful feedback to each other so that learning and development are constantly on the agenda. If you are an S/NVQ4 candidate you will see from the guidance that these are expectations of you, as detailed in Unit HSC43. But, regardless of whether or not you have line management responsibility, and whatever form your work and studying takes, it is still important to play a part in promoting an atmosphere within which people feel comfortable to give and receive constructive feedback.

Exercise 6.2

Whose feedback do you feel you could benefit from? Who are the key people in your work setting who could (or do) give you helpful feedback? What can you do to encourage such feedback?

6.3 Discrimination and oppression

Working within a value base involves recognising the value of all people, regardless of their race, colour, creed, gender, age, disability, sexual identity or other potential source of discrimination. In order to work within an ethical framework it is therefore necessary to continue to take account of discrimination and oppression. As we noted in Chapter 2, to ignore issues of discrimination and oppression leaves us in a position where we run the risk of exacerbating the situation – for example, by reinforcing existing patterns of discrimination.

Anti-discriminatory practice is based on the idea that we need to 'unlearn' what we have been brought up to take for granted – for example, in terms of differences in status between ethnic groups or different roles and expectations for men and women (Neil Thompson, 2006b). In view of this, it is vitally important that we continue to address issues of discrimination and oppression, for if we do not, we run the very serious risk of reverting unwittingly to old habits and relying once again on discriminatory assumptions or stereotypes, hence the very real need to 'remain alert' to such matters in our practice and in our interactions with others.

Remaining alert

Remaining alert to patterns of discrimination is a major challenge in social care, and one that has to be taken seriously if we are not to allow our work to contribute to maintaining or exacerbating existing inequalities. We therefore have to think carefully about how we can prevent any initial enthusiasm for promoting equality from dissipating over time.

The ways in which we can do this will differ from setting to setting and from individual to individual, but the following general guidelines should be of some help in trying to ensure that any gains made are not lost through old patterns of work and interaction reasserting themselves over time.

- *Team meeting agendas*: Discrimination and inequality can become standing items on team meeting agendas, although we have to guard against a tokenistic approach in which the issues are mentioned in passing just to make it look as though they are being taken seriously.

- *Ongoing training*: Many people have not even received initial training in anti-discriminatory practice and so it may be especially difficult to arrange opportunities for ongoing or advanced levels of training. However, where it is possible to make such arrangements, ongoing training can play a very important role. The issues involved are very complex and so opportunities to explore them in groups with the support of an experienced trainer can prove invaluable.

- *Support groups*: Many organisations have support groups linked to discrimination issues, either to address discrimination and oppression across the board or in relation to a particular form of oppression – for example, a black workers' support group.

- *Supervision*: These matters can and should be a topic that is discussed in supervision. Anti-discriminatory practice is a managerial and organisational responsibility as well as an individual professional one.

- *Review and evaluation*: In reviewing our work on an ongoing basis and evaluating it at the end of specific pieces of work we should have ample opportunity to consider whether or not we are taking account of equality issues and identify the steps we need to take if we are not doing so.

Underpinning all of this, of course, is the central concept of reflective practice, as discussed in Chapter 1. If we are taking the necessary steps to promote reflective practice, we will also be taking steps towards ensuring that discrimination and oppression remain firmly on the agenda, in so far as reflective practice should help us to avoid slipping into routinised patterns of practice which can be very uncritical and therefore dangerous.

Elegant challenging

A further aspect of 'remaining alert' to these important issues is to be able and willing to challenge discriminatory actions, attitudes or assumptions in others and inappropriate policies or institutional practices in organisations. If we do not challenge in this way, then we can be seen to collude with destructive or harmful practices that stand in the way of movements towards more egalitarian forms of practice. Once such an atmosphere of collusion has been established it can be very difficult indeed to break it down. Organisational cultures can be very firmly rooted and therefore very resistant to change (see Chapter 6 of Neil Thompson, 2003b, for a discussion of the part individuals and groups of staff can play in challenging and influencing organisational culture). In view of this, it is necessary to be quite skilled and strategic in the use of challenging if we are not to waste our efforts or, worse still, alienate people and thereby encourage them to become even more entrenched in their attitudes. For this reason, it is necessary to understand and develop what has become known as 'elegant challenging'.

Basically, elegant challenging refers to a tactful, subtle approach which is skilfully geared towards maximising the chances of having a positive influence on the other party. It is therefore important to ensure that any challenges we make are 'elegant' in so far as they are:

- *Carefully worded*: It does not usually pay to just blurt out how we feel about a particular matter. This can do more harm than good by 'getting people's back up'.

- *Timed appropriately*: There is a time and a place for challenging people. Sometimes the urge to challenge someone there and then can lead us into situations that cause a lot of embarrassment – and this then tends to act as a barrier to learning, as the person concerned will tend to concentrate on saving face in the situation rather than learning from it. A quiet word at a less threatening time will often be far more effective. However, it should be noted that this is not intended as a 'cop out'. It is no good deciding to tackle the issue at a more opportune moment and then not doing so – that is only likely to perpetuate the problem.

- *Constructive*: It is better to look for a constructive way forward rather than simply criticise someone. Personal attacks are unlikely to be helpful.

Exercise 6.3

Think about your current work situation. What opportunities do you have for challenging anything you consider to be discriminatory or oppressive? How would you ensure that you tackle such matters elegantly? What support could you expect to draw upon in dealing with such matters?

Another important issue to bear in mind when it comes to elegant challenging is to recognise that you may have got it wrong. For example, what sounds on the surface to be a discriminatory remark may not actually be so when you understand more about the circumstances. It is important not to jump to conclusions and assume that you 'know best'. In some respects, an overzealous, 'holier-than-thou' attitude can contribute enormously to attempts to develop anti-discriminatory practice being dismissed as extremism or 'political correctness'. An ill-considered, uncritical approach to questions of inequality, discrimination and oppression can not only fail to be effective but also actually make the situation worse – that is, it can do more harm than good (see Chapter 5 of Neil Thompson, 2003b). It therefore pays dividends to consider these matters carefully rather than rush in precipitously.

6.4 Professional development

The ideas underpinning continuous professional development (or 'CPD') were discussed in Chapter 1 in terms of the process of 'learning how to learn' (see also Chapter 8 of *People Skills*). Before proceeding, it would be wise for you to go back to that chapter now and re-read the section on learning how to learn. This should help you get the key issues fresh in your mind.

Why bother?

Many people work very hard to develop the basic competence they need to do their job reasonably well, but then pull back once they have achieved that level. They do not keep up the momentum of learning and development and prefer to 'rest on their laurels', relying on the knowledge and skills they already have without investing any time or energy into developing new ones. Of course, this is a dangerous approach in so far as it:

- Fails to keep up with new developments in law, policy, procedures, methods, techniques or perspectives. This means that standards of practice will steadily decline as they get more and more out of touch with the demands and developments of the wider world.

- Allows staff to become entrenched in routine, unthinking forms of practice as they are not able to adapt to new situations or the demands of new circumstances. Of course, the risk of errors is much higher when such an approach is adopted.

- Undermines morale and job satisfaction, as it becomes increasingly difficult to get any sense of achievement. This can then contribute significantly to higher levels of stress.

By contrast, continuous professional development can make a major contribution to:

- Confidence and a positive attitude towards learning;
- Opportunities to explore new ways of working, giving a broader 'repertoire' of skills and methods to draw on;
- Greater awareness of discrimination and oppression;
- A sound foundation for teamwork through learning together;
- Stimulation and motivation to carry on developing;
- More creative approaches to practice;
- Less likelihood of mistakes being made; and
- A higher level of morale and job satisfaction.

Keeping learning alive

Of course, establishing why it is important to make a commitment to continuous professional development is only part of the story. The other important part, of course, is working out what steps need to be taken to 'keep learning alive' and making sure they are actually taken.

One way of keeping learning on the agenda is to be aware of the barriers to learning that were discussed in Chapter 1, and being prepared to guard against them. Of course, there are many other ways of 'keeping learning alive', not least the following:

- *Supervision*: Being prepared to use supervision as an opportunity for learning and development is an important part of professional practice. See Chapter 7 of *People Skills*.

- *Training*: Opportunities to attend training courses vary considerably from one employing organisation to another. Some invest heavily in training while others seek to get away with the lowest level of training they can. However, what can be helpful is a proactive approach to training. This means seeking out training opportunities, rather than waiting for them to be brought to your attention.

- *Training follow up*: Lambert (1996) makes the important point that much of the benefit of training is lost because it is left behind in the training room and not transferred successfully to the work situation. What is needed, then, is the ability and willingness to use ideas in practice and therefore bring to life the discussions that take place on training courses. There is a need for an active approach. What is covered on a training course will not automatically apply itself to the work situation as if by magic – each of us has to make the effort to apply the insights gained. We have to use training as an aid to reflective practice rather than as an alternative to it.

- *Teamwork*: There is, of course, a great deal of learning to be gained from working together, drawing on the experience of those around you, discussing your approaches and constantly creating opportunities for new ideas and practices to be explored. Learning is not a competition where we have to show that we are better than the next person (although the school system can tend to encourage such a competitive attitude to learning). Learning can and should be a shared endeavour.

- *Reading*: A common misunderstanding is the notion that reading about social care issues is solely for people who are enrolled on courses. Professional practice involves keeping up to date with developments and broadening our understanding. It is therefore necessary to set aside a certain amount of time for reading relevant materials, even if this involves reading in our own time outside of work hours.

- *Using research*: New research developments are being reported all the time. Our knowledge base is therefore growing steadily – or it should be if we take the trouble to keep up to date with developments. This is not to say that every social care worker is expected to be an expert on all the latest research findings but there should at least be an attempt to read the summaries reported in the professional magazines and journals or quality newspapers.

This is not an exhaustive list, and of course, the opportunities will vary from place to place. The challenge, then, is to:

- Work out what opportunities for learning and development are available in your particular work setting;

- Be aware of the potential or actual barriers to learning and take the necessary steps to remove or avoid them;

- Identify which colleagues are likely to be a useful source of support and joint learning;

- Make sure that the pressures of work do not get in the way of taking the necessary time to continue to develop (see the next section on 'Self-management skills').

Exercise 6.4 is designed to help you with this challenge.

Exercise 6.4

In Chapter 1 you were asked to consider an Action Plan for Learning. Look back at that now (or look at it for the first time if you skipped the exercise first time round!) and consider how, as we approach the end of the book, you might want to change or build on that plan. Feel free to consult with others if you would find this helpful.

Self-management skills

One reason for not continuing to learn and develop that is often offered in defence is that of: 'I'm too busy, I haven't got time'. Another one is: 'My job is too stressful. I haven't got the luxury of being able to learn from what I do – I just have to get on with it'. While we can sympathise up to a point with these comments, we also have to recognise that they do not stand up to critical scrutiny when they are examined more closely.

The first statement relates to the skills of time and workload management, while the second relates to stress management – two very important sets of skills for social care workers. You should now read Chapters 2 and 3 of *People Skills*, which address these two topics.

After reading these two chapters, you should be able to appreciate that there is much that can be done to enhance our self-management or 'personal effectiveness' skills. It should also be clear that these skills should be helpful in enabling you to carry on learning and developing throughout your career.

6.5 Conclusion

The demands of social care are not static – they will continue to change and develop as circumstances change. New legislation and policies, new developments in theory and practice – these will all bring about a new set of pressures to respond to. It is therefore extremely important that we remain open to learning, that we continue to think about:

- what we are doing;
- why we are doing it;
- whether we are doing it well; and
- what we can learn from doing it.

It should be clear, then, that the issues discussed in this chapter are very important as part of the foundations of high-quality professional practice in social care. It is therefore to be hoped that you will be able to take them on board and rise to the challenge of ensuring that your work:

- is evaluated so that you can build on strengths and seek to turn weaknesses into strengths;
- challenges discrimination and oppression and respects the ethical requirements of professional practice;
- enables you to carry on learning and developing.

We are confident you have the resourcefulness to achieve these three aims and we wish you well in your endeavours to do so.

Guide to Further Learning

Part One: Suggestions for Further Reading

Chapter 1: Learning from Experience

Gould, N. and Taylor, I. (eds) (1996) *Reflective Learning for Social Work*, Aldershot, Arena.

Kolb, O. (1984) *Experiential Learning*, Englewood Cliffs, NJ, Prentice-Hall.

Malone, C., Forbat, L., Robb, M. and Seden, J. (2005) *Relating Experience: Stories from Health and Social Care*, London, Routledge.

Martyn, H. (ed.) (2000) *Developing Reflective Practice: Making Sense of Social Work in a World of Change*, Bristol, Policy Press.

Peel, M. (2003) 'Managing Professional Development', in Seden and Reynolds (2003).

Reynolds, J., Henderson, J., Seden, J., Charlseworth, J. and Bullman, A. (eds) (2003) *The Managing Care Reader*, London, Routledge – Part 4 of this reader focuses on managing for a learning and developing organisation.

Schön, D. (1983) *The Reflective Practitioner*, Aldershot, Ashgate. A classic text that has proven very influential.

Thompson, N. (2000) *Theory and Practice in Human Services*, 2nd edn, Buckingham, Open University Press.

Thompson, N. (2006a) *Promoting Workplace Learning*, Bristol, The Policy Press.

Thompson, N. and Bates, J. (1996) *Learning from Other Disciplines: Lessons from Nurse Education and Management Theory*, Norwich, University of East Anglia Monographs.

Waldman, J. (1999) *Help Yourself to Learning at Work*, Lyme Regis, Russell House Publishing.

Chapter 2: The Value Base of Social Care

Banks, S. (2005) *Values and Ethics in Social Work*, 3rd edn, Basingstoke, Palgrave Macmillan. Provides a useful overview of values, as do:

Kallen, E. (2004) *Social Inequality and Social Justice: A Human Rights Perspective*, Basingstoke, Palgrave Macmillan.

Lewis, G. (ed) (2004) *Citizenship: Personal Lives and Social Policy*, Bristol, The Policy Press.

Moss, B. (2005) *Religion and Spirituality*, Lyme Regis, Russell House Publishing.

Moss, B. (2006) *Values*, Lyme Regis, Russell House Publishing.

Preston-Shoot, M. (1998) *Acting Fairly: Working Within the Law to Promote Equal Opportunities in Education and Training*, London, CCETSW. An excellent overview of the law relating to discrimination.

Pritchard, J. (2001) *Good Practice with Vulnerable Adults*, London, Jessica Kingsley.

Shardlow, S. (2002) 'Values, Ethics and Social Work', in Adams et al. (2002a) is a short chapter, but none the less a useful one.

Thompson, N. (2003b) *Promoting Equality: Challenging Discrimination and Oppression*, 2nd edn, Basingstoke, Palgrave Macmillan. A more advanced discussion of discrimination and oppression.

Swain, J., French, S., Barnes, C. and Thomas, C. (eds) (2004) *Disabling Barriers – Enabling Environments*, 2nd edn, London, Sage.

Thompson, N. (2005) *Understanding Social Work: Preparing for Practice*, 2nd edn, Basingstoke, Palgrave.

Thompson, N. (2006b) *Anti-Discriminatory Practice*, 4th edn, Basingstoke, Palgrave Macmillan. An introductory text that goes into some detail about the importance of anti-discriminatory practice and what is involved in promoting it.

Chapter 3: Working in Partnership

Adams, R. (2003) *Social Work and Empowerment*, 3rd edn, Basingstoke, Palgrave Macmillan.

Carnwell, R. and Buchanan, J. (eds) (2005) *Effective Practice in Health and Social Care: A Partnership Approach*, Maidenhead, Open University Press.

Crimmens, D. and Pitts, J. (2000) *Positive Residential Practice: Learning the Lessons of the 1990s*, Lyme Regis, Russell House Publishing.

Harrison, R., Mann, G., Murphy, M., Taylor, A. and Thompson, N. (2002) *Partnership Made Painless*, Lyme Regis, Russell House Publishing. Geared towards multiagency partnerships rather than worker-service user or worker-worker partnerships, but useful none the less.

Kemshall, H. and Littlechild, R. (eds) (2000) *User Involvement in Social Care: Research Informing Practice*, London, Jessica Kingsley.

Leathard, A. (ed) (2003) *Interprofessional Collaboration: From Policy to Practice in Health and Social Care*, Hove, Brunner-Routledge.

Onyett S. (2003) *Teamworking in Mental Health*, Basingstoke, Palgrave Macmillan.

Roulstone, A., Hudson, V., Kearney, J. and Martin, A. with Warren, J. (2006) *Working Together: Carer Participation in England, Wales and Northern Ireland*, London, Social Care Institute for Excellence.

Thompson, N. (2003a) *Communication and Language: A Handbook of Theory and Practice*, Basingstoke, Palgrave Macmillan.

Thompson, S. (2002) *From Where I'm Sitting*, Lyme Regis, Russell House Publishing. A training manual emphasising the importance of understanding the service user's perspective when working with older people.

Thompson, N. (2006d) *Power and Empowerment*, Lyme Regis, Russell House Publishing.

Chapter 4: Understanding Assessment

Brearley, P. (1982) *Risk and Social Work*, London, Routledge.

Department for Education and Skills (2006) *Common Assessment Framework: Managers' Guide/Practitioners' Guide*, downloadable from www.everychildmatters.gov.uk/re-sources-and-practice/IG00063

Horwath, J. (ed) (2001) *The Child's World: Assessing Children in Need*, London, Jessica Kingsley.

Milner, J. and O'Byrne, P. (2002) *Assessment in Social Work*, 2nd edn, Basingstoke, Palgrave Macmillan. A very useful introductory text.

O' Sullivan, P. (2002) 'Managing Risk in Decision Making' in Adams et al. (2002b).

Parker, J. and Bradley, G. (2003) *Social Work Practice: Assessment, Planning, Intervention and Review*, Exeter, Learning Matters.

Parsloe, P. (1999) *Risk Assessment in Social Care and Social Work*, London, Jessica Kingsley.

Parton, N., Thorpe, D. and Wattam, C. (eds) (1997) *Child Protection: Risk and the Moral Order*, London, Macmillan – now Palgrave Macmillan.

Thompson, N. (2002a) *People Skills*, 2nd edn, Basingstoke, Palgrave Macmillan.

Chapter 5: Planning Responses

Carr, S. (2004) *Has Service User Participation Made a Difference to Social Care Services?*, London, Social Care Institute for Excellence.

Durkin, K. (1995) *Developmental Social Psychology: From Infancy to Old Age*, Oxford, Blackwell.

Egan, G. (2004) *The Skilled Helper: A Problem-Management and Opportunity Development Approach to Helping*, 7th edn, Thompson Learning.

Parker, J. and Bradley, G. (2003) *Social Work Practice: Assessment, Planning, Intervention and Review*, Exeter, Learning Matters.

The Older People's Steering Group (2004) *Older People Shaping Policy and Practice*, York, Joseph Rowntree Foundation.

Thompson, N. (1991) *Crisis Intervention Revisited*, Birmingham, Pepar.

Books relating to loss

Corr, C.A., Nabe, C.M. and Corr, D. (2005) *Death and Dying, Life and Living*, 5th edn, New York, Thomson Learning.

Currer, C. (2001) *Responding to Grief: Dying, Bereavement and Social Care*, Basingstoke, Palgrave Macmillan.

Dickenson, D., Johnson, M. and Katz, J.S. (eds) (2000) *Death, Dying and Bereavement*, London, Sage.

Doka, K. (ed) (1995) *Children Mourning, Mourning Children*, Washington DC, Hospice Foundation of America/Taylor and Francis.

Neimeyer, R.A. (ed.) (2001) *Meaning Reconstruction and the Experience of Loss*, Washington DC, American Psychological Association.

Parkes, C.M., Laungani, P. and Young, B. (eds) (1997) *Death and Bereavement Across Cultures*, London, Routledge.

Riches, G. and Dawson, P. (2000) *An Intimate Loneliness: Supporting Bereaved Parents and Siblings*, Buckingham, Open University Press.

Stroebe, M., Stroebe, W. and Hansson, R.O. (eds) (1993) *Handbook of Bereavement: Theory, Research and Intervention*, Cambridge University Press – a little old now but still a useful and comprehensive volume.

Thompson, N. (ed) (2002) *Loss and Grief: A Guide for Human Services Practitioners*, Basingstoke, Palgrave Macmillan.

Chapter 6: Evaluation and Development

Everitt, A. and Hardiker, P. (1996) *Evaluating for Good Practice*, London, Macmillan – now Palgrave Macmillan.

Pinnock, M. and Dimmock, B. (2003) 'Managing for Outcomes', in Henderson and Atkinson (2003).

Shaw, I. and Lishman, J. (1999) *Evaluation and Social Work Practice*, London, Sage.

Sheldon, B. and Chilvers, R. (2000) *Evidence-based Social Care: A Study of Prospects and Problems*, Lyme Regis, Russell House Publishing.

Shemmings, D. and Shemmings, Y. (2003) 'Supporting Evidence-based Practice and Research-mindedness', in Seden and Reynolds (2003).

Subhra, G. (2001) 'Reclaiming the Evaluation Agenda', in Factor et al. (2001).

Thompson, N. (2000a) *Theory and Practice in Human Services*, 2nd edn, Buckingham, Open University Press.

Thompson, N. (2006a) *Promoting Workplace Learning*, Bristol, The Policy Press.

Thompson, N. and Bates, J. (1996) *Learning from Other Disciplines: Lessons from Nurse Education and Management Theory*, Norwich, University of East Anglia Monographs.

Waldman, J. (1999) *Help Yourself to Learning at Work*, Lyme Regis, Russell House Publishing.

Walker, I., Nutley, S., Percy-smith, J., McNeish, D. and Frost, S. (2004) *Improving the Use of Research in Social Care Practice* – downloadable from the SCIE website: www.scie.org.uk/publications/knowledgereviews.

Part Two: Websites

You may find the following sites useful in their own right and as gateways to other sources of information. Please note that the site details were correct at the time of writing, but may change over time.

General

Community Care magazine   www.community-care.co.uk
Social Care Online   www.scie-socialcareonline.org.uk
Learning support   www.support4learning.org.uk
Info for Local Government   www.info4local.gov.uk

INTUTE   www.intute.ac/uk/socialsciences/socialwelfare
Human solutions (staff support)   www.humansolutions.org.uk

Specific service areas
Age Concern   www.ageconcern.org.uk
The Alzheimer's Disease Society   www.alzheimers.org.uk
Better Government for Older People   www.bgop.org.uk
Barnardo's   www.barnardos.org.uk
National Children's Bureau   www.ncb.org.uk
National Youth Advocacy Service   www.nyas.net
People First (run by people with Learning Disabilities)   www.peoplefirst.org.uk
Campaign for Racial Equality   www.cre.gov.uk
Royal National Institute for Deaf People   www.rnid.org.uk
Deaf community   www.deaf.com
Royal National Institute for the Blind   www.rnib.org.uk
Disability Rights Commission   www.drc-gb.org
MIND (mental health)   www.mind.org.uk
Nimhe (mental health)   www.nimhe.org.uk
Stonewall (gay and lesbian rights)   www.stonewall.org.uk
Protection of Vulnerable Adults (POVA)   www.doh.gov.uk (enter POVA into search)

References

Adams, R. (1994) *Skilled Work with People*, London, Collins Educational.

Adams, R. (2003) *Social Work and Empowerment*, 3rd edn, Basingstoke, Palgrave Macmillan.

Adams, R. (2002) 'Social Work Processes', in Adams *et al.* (2002a).

Adams, R., Dominelli, L. and Payne, M. (eds) (2002a) *Social Work: Themes, Issues and Critical Debates*, 2nd edn, Basingstoke, Palgrave Macmillan.

Adams, R., Dominelli, L. and Payne, M. (eds) (2002b) *Critical Practice in Social Work*, Basingstoke, Palgrave Macmillan.

Banks, S. (2005) *Ethics and Values in Social Work*, 2nd edn, Basingstoke, Palgrave Macmillan.

Biestek, F.P. (1961) *The Casework Relationship*, London, Allen and Unwin.

Brearley, P. (1982) *Risk and Social Work*, London, Routledge.

Carson, D. (1996) 'Risking Legal Repercussions', in Kemshall and Pritchard (1996).

Egan, G. (2004) *The Skilled Helper: A Problem-Management and Opportunity Development Approach to Helping*, 7th edn, New York, Thomson Learning.

Erikson, E. (1977) *Childhood and Society*, London, Paladin.

Factor, F., Chauhan, V. and Pitts, J. (eds) (2001) *The RHP Companion to Working with Young People*, Lyme Regis, Russell House Publishing.

Goffman, E. (1959) *The Presentation of Self in Everyday Life*, New York, Doubleday Anchor.

Henderson, J. and Atkinson, D. (eds) (2003) *Managing Care in Context*, London, Routledge.

Hughes, B. (1995) *Older People and Community Care: Critical Theory and Practice*, Buckingham, Open University Press.

Kemshall, H. and Pritchard, J. (eds) (1996) *Good Practice in Risk Assessment*, London, Jessica Kingsley.

Kolb, D. (1984) *Experiential Learning*, Englewood Cliffs, NJ, Prentice-Hall.

Lambert, T. (1996) *Key Management Solutions*, London, Pitman.

Lewis, D. and Sargeant, M. (2004) *Essentials of Employment Law*, 8th edn, London, Chartered Institute of Personnel and Development.

Littlechild, R. and Blakeney, J. (1996) 'Risk and Older People', in Kemshall and Pritchard (1996).

More, W. (1997) *The New ABC of Handling Aggression*, Birmingham, Pepar.

Oliver, M. (1996) *Understanding Disability: From Theory to Practice*, London, Macmillan – now Palgrave Macmillan.

Parekh, B. (2006) *Rethinking Multiculturalism: Cultural Diversity and Political Theory*, 2nd edn, Basingstoke, Palgrave Macmillan.

Parton, N., Thorpe, D. and Wattam, C. (eds) (1997) *Child Protection: Risk and the Moral Order*, London, Macmillan – now Palgrave Macmillan.

Payne, M. (2005) *Social Work Theory: A Critical Introduction*, 3rd edn, Basingstoke, Palgrave Macmillan.

Pilkington, A. (2003) *Racial Disadvantage and Ethnic Diversity in Britain*, Basingstoke, Palgrave Macmillan.

Rogers, C. (1961) *On Becoming a Person*, London, Constable.

Shaw, I. (1996) *Evaluating in Practice*, Aldershot, Arena.

Seden, J. and Reynolds, J. (eds) (2003) *Managing Care in Practice*, London, Routledge.

Smith, A. and Russell, J. (1993) 'Using Critical Incidents in Nurse Education', *Nurse Education Today* 11.

Swain, J., French, S., Barnes, C. and Thomas, C. (eds) (2004) *Disabling Barriers – Enabling Environments*, London, Sage.

Thompson, N. (1991) *Crisis Intervention Revisited*, Birmingham, Pepar.

Thompson, N. (2000) *Theory and Practice in Human Services*, 2nd edn, Buckingham, Open University Press.

Thompson, N. (2002a) *People Skills*, 2nd edn, Basingstoke, Palgrave Macmillan.

Thompson, N. (ed) (2002b) *Loss and Grief: A Guide for Human Services Practitioners*, Basingstoke, Palgrave Macmillan.

Thompson, N. (2003a) *Communication and Language: A Handbook of Theory and Practice*, Basingstoke, Palgrave Macmillan.

Thompson, N. (2003b) *Promoting Equality: Challenging Discrimination and Oppression*, 2nd edn, Basingstoke, Palgrave Macmillan.

Thompson, N. (2006a) *Promoting Workplace Learning*, Bristol, The Policy Press.

Thompson, N. (2006b) *Anti-Discriminatory Practice*, 4th edn, Basingstoke, Palgrave Macmillan.

Thompson, N. (2006c) *People Problems*, Basingstoke, Palgrave Macmillan.

Thompson, N. (2006d) *Power and Empowerment*, Lyme Regis, Russell House Publishing.

Thompson, N., Murphy, M. and Stradling, S. (1994) *Dealing with Stress*, London, Macmillan – now Palgrave Macmillan.

Thompson, N., Murphy, M. and Stradling, S. (1996) *Meeting the Stress Challenge*, Lyme Regis, Russell House Publishing.

Thompson, S. (2002) *From Where I'm Sitting: A Manual for Those Working with Older People in the Social Care Sector*, Lyme Regis, Russell House Publishing.

Thompson, S. (2005) *Age Discrimination*, Lyme Regis, Russell House Publishing.

Appendix

Health and social care level 4

Core units

UNIT HSC41	Use and develop methods and systems to communicate record and report.
HSC41a	Identify methods and systems to promote effective communication and engagement with individuals and key people.
HSC41b	Develop and use communication methods and systems to promote effective communication.
HSC41c	Evaluate communication methods and systems.
HSC41	Maintain and share evidence-based records and reports.
UNIT HSC42	Contribute to the development and maintenance of healthy and safe practices in the working environment.
HSC42a	Contribute to monitoring compliance with health, safety and security regulations and requirements.
HSC42b	Contribute to the development of systems to manage risk to self, staff and others.
HSC42c	Contribute to the development of health, safety and security policies, procedures and practices.
UNIT HSC43	Take responsibility for the continuing professional development of self and others.
UNIT HSC44	(Children and young people route) Develop practice which promotes the involvement, well-being and protection of children and young people.
UNIT HSC45	(Adults route) Develop practices which promote choice, well-being and protection of all individuals.

Children and young people specific

HSC46	Independently represent and advocate with, and on behalf of, children and young people.
HSC47	Help parents and carers to acquire and use skills to protect and take care of children and young people.
HSC48	Demonstrate a style of leadership that ensures an organisational culture of open and participatory management and practice.
HSC49	Develop and maintain an environment which safeguards and protects children and young people.

Adults specific

HSC410   Advocate with, and on behalf of, individuals, families, carers, groups and communities.

HSC411   Manage a service which achieves the best possible outcomes for the individual.

HSC412   Ensure individuals and groups are supported appropriately when experiencing significant life events and transitions.

Generic

HSC413   Manage requests for health and care services

HSC414   Assess individual needs and preferences

HSC415   Produce, evaluate and amend service delivery plans to meet individual needs and preferences

HSC416   Develop, implement and review care plans with individuals

HSC417   Assess individuals' mental health and related needs

HSC418   Work with individuals with mental health needs to negotiate and agree plans for addressing those needs

HSC419   Provide advice and information to those who enquire about mental health needs and related services

HSC420   Promote leisure opportunities and activities for individuals

HSC421   Promote employment, training and education opportunities for individuals

HSC422   Promote housing opportunities for individuals

HSC423   Assist individuals at formal hearings

HSC424   Supervise methadone consumption

HSC425   Support people who are providing homes for individuals and/or children and young people

HSC426   Empower families, carers and others to support individuals

HSC427   Assess the needs of carers and families

HSC428   Develop, implement and review programmes of support for carers and families

HSC429   Work with groups to promote individual growth, development and independence

HSC430   Support the protection of individuals, key people and others

HSC431   Support individuals where abuse has been disclosed

HSC432   Enable families to address issues with individuals' behaviour

HSC433   Develop joint working agreements and practices and review their effectiveness

HSC434   Maintain and manage records and reports

HSC435   Manage the development and direction of the provision

HSC436   Promote and manage a quality provision

HSC437   Promote your organisation and its services to stakeholders

HSC438	Develop and disseminate information and advice about substance use, health and social well-being
HSC439	Contribute to the development of organisational policy and practice
HSC440	Support effective governance
HSC441	Invite tenders and award contracts
HSC442	Monitor and evaluate the quality, outcomes and cost-effectiveness of substance misuse services
HSC443	Procure services for individuals
HSC444	Contribute to the selection, recruitment and retention of staff to develop a quality service
HSC445	Recruit and place volunteers
HSC446	Manage a dispersed workforce to meet the needs and preferences of individuals at home
HSC447	Represent the agency in courts and formal hearings
HSC448	Provide and obtain information at courts and formal hearings
HSC449	Represent one's own agency at other agencies' meetings
HSC450	Develop risk management plans to support individuals' independence and daily living within their homes
HSC451	Lead teams to support a quality provision
HSC452	Contribute to the development, maintenance and evaluation of systems to promote the rights, responsibilities, equality and diversity of individuals.